NO FEAR SHAKESPEARE

NO FEAR SHAKESPEARE

As You Like It

The Comedy of Errors

Hamlet

Henry IV, Parts One and Two

Henry V

Julius Caesar

King Lear

Macbeth

The Merchant of Venice

A Midsummer Night's Dream

Much Ado About Nothing

Othello

Richard III

Romeo and Juliet

Sonnets

The Taming of the Shrew

The Tempest

Twelfth Night

NO FEAR SHAKESPEARE

TWELFTH NIGHT

Edited by
John Crowther

SPARK
NOTES

SPARKNOTES is a registered trademark of SparkNotes LLC.

Spark Publishing
A Division of Barnes & Noble, Inc.
120 Fifth Avenue
New York, NY 10011
www.sparknotes.com

Please submit all comments and questions or report errors to www.sparknotes.com/errors

ISBN: 978-1-5866-3851-1

Library of Congress Cataloging-in-Publication Data

Shakespeare, William, 1564–1616.
Twelfth Night / edited by John Crowther.
    p. cm.—(No fear Shakespeare)
  Summary: Presents the original text of Shakespeare's play side by side with a modern
version, with marginal notes and explanations and full descriptions of each character.
  ISBN 1-58663-851-3 (pbk.) ISBN 1-4114-0049-6 (hc.)
  1. Survival after airplane accidents, shipwrecks, etc.—Drama. 2. Brothers and sisters—
Drama. 3. Illyria—Drama. 4. Twins—Drama. [1. Shakespeare, William, 1564–1616.
Twelfth Night. 2. Plays. 3. English literature—History and criticism.]
I. Crowther, John (John C.) II. Title.
PR2837 .A2 C76 2003
822.3'3—dc22
                                                    200301566

Printed and bound in the United States of America

25

There's matter in these sighs, these profound heaves.
You must translate: 'tis fit we understand them.

(Hamlet, 4.1.1–2)

FEAR NOT.

Have you ever found yourself looking at a Shakespeare play, then down at the footnotes, then back at the play, and still not understanding? You know what the individual words mean, but they don't add up. SparkNotes' *No Fear Shakespeare* will help you break through all that. Put the pieces together with our easy-to-read translations. Soon you'll be reading Shakespeare's own words fearlessly—and actually enjoying it.

No Fear Shakespeare puts Shakespeare's language side-by-side with a facing-page translation into modern English—the kind of English people actually speak today. When Shakespeare's words make your head spin, our translation will help you sort out what's happening, who's saying what, and why.

TWELFTH NIGHT

Characters ix

ACT ONE
Scene 1.........................2
Scene 2.........................6
Scene 3.........................12
Scene 4.........................26
Scene 5.........................30

ACT TWO
Scene 1.........................60
Scene 2.........................64
Scene 3.........................68
Scene 4.........................86
Scene 5.........................98

ACT THREE
Scene 1.........................118
Scene 2.........................134
Scene 3.........................142
Scene 4.........................148

ACT FOUR
Scene 1.........................184
Scene 2.........................192

ACT FIVE
Scene 1.........................208

CHARACTERS

Viola—A young woman of aristocratic birth, and the play's pro-
tagonist. Washed up on the shore of Illyria when her ship is
wrecked in a storm, Viola decides to make her own way in the
world. She disguises herself as a young man, calling herself
"Cesario," and becomes a page to Duke Orsino. She ends up
falling in love with Orsino—even as Olivia, the woman Orsino is courting, falls in love with Cesario. Thus, Viola finds
that her clever disguise has entrapped her: she cannot tell
Orsino that she loves him, and she cannot tell Olivia why she,
as Cesario, cannot love *her*. Viola's poignant plight is the cen-
tral conflict in the play.

Orsino—A powerful nobleman in the country of Illyria. Orsino is
lovesick for the beautiful Lady Olivia, but finds himself
becoming more and more fond of his handsome new page boy,
Cesario, who is actually a woman—Viola. Orsino is a vehicle
through whom Shakespeare explores the absurdity of love. A
supreme egotist, Orsino mopes around complaining how
heartsick he is over Olivia, when it is clear that he is chiefly in
love with the idea of being in love and enjoys making a spec-
tacle of himself.

Olivia—A wealthy, beautiful, and noble Illyrian lady. Olivia is
courted by Orsino and Sir Andrew Aguecheek, but to each of
them she insists that she is in mourning for her recently
deceased brother and will not marry for seven years. Olivia
and Orsino are similar characters in that each seems to enjoy
wallowing in his or her own misery. Viola's arrival in the masculine guise of Cesario enables Olivia to break free of her self-
indulgent melancholy.

Sebastian—Viola's lost twin brother. When Sebastian arrives in Illyria, traveling with Antonio, his close friend and protector, he discovers that many people seem to think that they know him. Furthermore, the beautiful Lady Olivia, whom Sebastian has never met, wants to marry him.

Malvolio—The straitlaced steward—or head servant—in the household of Lady Olivia. Malvolio is very efficient but also very self-righteous, and he has a poor opinion of drinking, singing, and fun. His priggishness and haughty attitude earn him the enmity of Sir Toby, Sir Andrew, and Maria, who play a cruel trick on him, making him believe that Olivia is in love with him. In his fantasies about marrying his mistress, Malvolio reveals a powerful ambition to rise above his social class.

Fool—The clown, or court jester, of Olivia's household. The Fool, also known as Feste, moves between Olivia's and Orsino's homes, earning his living by making pointed jokes, singing old songs, being generally witty, and offering good advice cloaked under a layer of foolishness. In spite of being a professional fool, Feste often seems the wisest character in the play.

Sir Toby Belch—Olivia's uncle. Olivia lets Sir Toby live with her but does not approve of his rowdy behavior, practical jokes, heavy drinking, late-night carousing, or friends (specifically the idiotic Sir Andrew). But Sir Toby has an ally—and eventually a mate—in Olivia's sharp-witted servingwoman, Maria. Together, they bring about the triumph of fun and disorder, which Sir Toby embodies, and the humiliation of the controlling, self-righteous Malvolio.

Maria—Olivia's clever, daring young serving-woman. Maria is remarkably similar to her antagonist, Malvolio, who harbors aspirations of rising in the world through marriage. However, Maria succeeds where Malvolio fails—perhaps because she is more in tune than Malvolio with the anarchic, topsy-turvy spirit that animates the play.

Sir Andrew—A friend of Sir Toby's. Sir Andrew Aguecheek attempts to court Olivia, but he doesn't stand a chance. He thinks that he is witty, brave, young, and good at languages and dancing, but he is actually a complete idiot.

Antonio—A man who rescues Sebastian after his shipwreck. Antonio has become very fond of Sebastian, caring for him, accompanying him to Illyria, and furnishing him with money—all because of a love so strong that it seems to be romantic in nature. When the principal characters marry at the end of the play, Antonio is left out, his love for Sebastian unrequited.

Valentine and **Curio**—Two gentlemen who work for Duke Orsino.

Fabian—A servant in Olivia's household. He assists Maria and Sir Toby in their plot to humiliate Malvolio.

Captain—The sea captain who rescues Viola after the shipwreck. He helps Viola become a page to Duke Orsino and keeps her identity a secret.

ACT ONE
SCENE 1

Enter ORSINO, CURIO, *and other lords; Musicians playing*

ORSINO
If music be the food of love, play on.
Give me excess of it that, surfeiting,
The appetite may sicken, and so die.
That strain again, it had a dying fall.
Oh, it came o'er my ear like the sweet sound,
That breathes upon a bank of violets,
Stealing and giving odor. Enough, no more.
'Tis not so sweet now as it was before.
O spirit of love, how quick and fresh art thou,
That, notwithstanding thy capacity
Receiveth as the sea, nought enters there,
Of what validity and pitch soe'er,
But falls into abatement and low price
Even in a minute. So full of shapes is fancy
That it alone is high fantastical.

CURIO
Will you go hunt, my lord?

ORSINO
What, Curio?

CURIO
The hart.

ORSINO
Why, so I do, the noblest that I have.
Oh, when mine eyes did see Olivia first,
Methought she purged the air of pestilence.
That instant was I turned into a hart,
And my desires, like fell and cruel hounds,
E'er since pursue me.

ACT ONE
SCENE 1

ORSINO, CURIO, *and other lords enter with musicians playing for them.*

ORSINO

If it's true that music makes people more in love, keep playing. Give me too much of it, so I'll get sick of it and stop loving. Play that part again! It sounded sad. Oh, it sounded like a sweet breeze blowing gently over a bank of violets, taking their scent with it. That's enough. Stop. It doesn't sound as sweet as it did before. Oh, love is so restless! It makes you want everything, but it makes you sick of things a minute later, no matter how good they are. Love is so vivid and fantastical that nothing compares to it.

CURIO

Do you want to go hunting, my lord?

ORSINO

Hunting what, Curio?

CURIO

The hart.

hart = male deer

ORSINO

That's what I'm doing—only it's *my* heart that's being hunted. Oh, when I first saw Olivia, it seemed like she made the air around her sweeter and purer. In that instant I was transformed into a hart, and my desire for her has hounded me like a pack of vicious dogs.

Enter VALENTINE

How now! What news from her?

VALENTINE
So please my lord, I might not be admitted,
But from her handmaid do return this answer:
25   The element itself, till seven years' heat,
Shall not behold her face at ample view,
But like a cloistress, she will veiled walk
And water once a day her chamber round
With eye-offending brine—all this to season
30   A brother's dead love, which she would keep fresh
And lasting in her sad remembrance.

ORSINO
O, she that hath a heart of that fine frame
To pay this debt of love but to a brother,
How will she love, when the rich golden shaft
35   Hath killed the flock of all affections else
That live in her, when liver, brain, and heart,
These sovereign thrones, are all supplied, and filled
Her sweet perfections with one self king!
Away before me to sweet beds of flowers.
40   Love thoughts lie rich when canopied with bowers.

Exeunt

VALENTINE *enters.*

What's going on? What have you heard from her?

VALENTINE

I'm sorry, but they wouldn't let me in. But I got the following answer from her handmaid. Olivia's not going to show her face for the next seven years—not even to the sky itself. Instead, she'll go around veiled like a nun, and once a day she'll water her room with tears. She's doing this out of love for her dead brother, whom she wants to keep fresh in her memory forever.

ORSINO

Oh, if she loves her brother this much, think how she'll love me when I finally win her over and make her forget all her other attachments! Her mind and heart will be ruled by one man alone—me! Take me to the garden. I need a beautiful place to sit and think about love.

They exit.

ACT 1, SCENE 2

Enter VIOLA, *a* CAPTAIN, *and sailors*

VIOLA
What country, friends, is this?

CAPTAIN
                                        This is Illyria, lady.

VIOLA
And what should I do in Illyria?
My brother he is in Elysium.
Perchance he is not drown'd.—What think you, sailors?

CAPTAIN
5   It is perchance that you yourself were saved.

VIOLA
O, my poor brother! And so perchance may he be.

CAPTAIN
True, madam. And, to comfort you with chance,
Assure yourself, after our ship did split,
When you and those poor number saved with you
10   Hung on our driving boat, I saw your brother,
Most provident in peril, bind himself,
Courage and hope both teaching him the practice,
To a strong mast that lived upon the sea,
Where, like Arion on the dolphin's back,
15   I saw him hold acquaintance with the waves
So long as I could see.

VIOLA
(giving him money)
                                        For saying so, there's gold.
Mine own escape unfoldeth to my hope,
Whereto thy speech serves for authority,
The like of him. Know'st thou this country?

CAPTAIN
20   Ay, madam, well, for I was bred and born
Not three hours' travel from this very place.

ACT 1, SCENE 2

VIOLA, *a* CAPTAIN, *and sailors enter.*

VIOLA

What country is this, friends?

CAPTAIN

This is Illyria, lady.

VIOLA

And what am I supposed to do in Illyria? My brother is in heaven. Or maybe there's a chance he didn't drown.—What do you think, sailors?

CAPTAIN

It was a total fluke that you yourself were saved.

VIOLA

Oh, my poor brother! But maybe by some fluke he was saved too.

CAPTAIN

Arion was a Greek poet who was saved from drowning by a dolphin.

It's possible, ma'am. Don't give up yet. When our ship was wrecked and you and a few other survivors were clinging onto our lifeboat, I saw your brother tie himself to a big mast floating in the sea. He was acting resourcefully and courageously in a dangerous situation. For as long as I could see him, he stayed afloat on the waves like Arion on the dolphin's back.

VIOLA

(giving him money) Thank you for saying that—here's some money to express my gratitude. Since I survived, it's easier for me to imagine he survived too, and what you say gives me a reason to hope for the best. Do you know this area we're in?

CAPTAIN

Yes, ma'am, I know it well. I was born and raised less than three hours from here.

VIOLA
Who governs here?

CAPTAIN
A noble duke, in nature
As in name.

VIOLA
What is his name?

CAPTAIN
Orsino.

VIOLA
Orsino. I have heard my father name him.
25   He was a bachelor then.

CAPTAIN
And so is now, or was so very late.
For but a month ago I went from hence,
And then 'twas fresh in murmur—as, you know,
What great ones do the less will prattle of—
30   That he did seek the love of fair Olivia.

VIOLA
What's she?

CAPTAIN
A virtuous maid, the daughter of a count
That died some twelvemonth since, then leaving her
In the protection of his son, her brother,
35   Who shortly also died, for whose dear love,
They say, she hath abjured the company
And sight of men.

VIOLA
Oh, that I served that lady
And might not be delivered to the world,
Till I had made mine own occasion mellow,
40   What my estate is.

CAPTAIN
That were hard to compass,
Because she will admit no kind of suit,
No, not the duke's.

VIOLA

Who's the ruler here?

CAPTAIN

A duke who is noble in name and character.

VIOLA

What's his name?

CAPTAIN

Orsino.

VIOLA

Orsino. I've heard my father mention him. When I first heard about him, he was still a bachelor.

CAPTAIN

He's still a bachelor, or at least he was a month ago, when I left. But there was a rumor—you know, people always gossip about royalty—that he was in love with the beautiful Olivia.

VIOLA

Who's she?

CAPTAIN

A virtuous young woman, the daughter of a count who died last year. Her brother had custody of her for a while, but then he died too. They say she's totally sworn off men now, in memory of her brother.

VIOLA

I wish I could work for that lady! It'd be a good way to hide from the world until the time was right to identify myself.

CAPTAIN

That would be hard to do. She won't allow anyone in to see her, not even the duke's messengers.

VIOLA
There is a fair behavior in thee, captain,
And though that nature with a beauteous wall
45   Doth oft close in pollution, yet of thee
I will believe thou hast a mind that suits
With this thy fair and outward character.
I prithee—and I'll pay thee bounteously—
Conceal me what I am, and be my aid
50   For such disguise as haply shall become
The form of my intent. I'll serve this duke.
Thou shall present me as an eunuch to him.
It may be worth thy pains, for I can sing
And speak to him in many sorts of music
55   That will allow me very worth his service.
What else may hap to time I will commit.
Only shape thou thy silence to my wit.

CAPTAIN
Be you his eunuch, and your mute I'll be.
When my tongue blabs, then let mine eyes not see.

VIOLA
60   I thank thee. Lead me on.

Exeunt

VIOLA

You seem to be a good person, captain, and although people who look beautiful are often corrupt inside, I believe that you have a beautiful mind to go with your good looks and manners. Please—and I'll pay you plenty for this—help me conceal my identity, and find me the right disguise so I can look the way I want. I want to be this Duke's servant. You'll introduce me to him as a eunuch. You won't be wasting your time, because I really can sing and talk to him about many different kinds of music, so he'll be happy to have me in his service. Only time will tell what will happen after that—just please keep quiet about what I'm trying to do.

CAPTAIN

I won't say a word. You can be a eunuch, but I'll be mute. I swear on my life I won't tell your secret.

VIOLA

Thank you. Show me the way.

They exit.

ACT 1, SCENE 3

Enter SIR TOBY BELCH *and* MARIA

SIR TOBY BELCH
What a plague means my niece, to take the death of her
brother thus? I am sure care's an enemy to life.

MARIA
By my troth, Sir Toby, you must come in earlier o' nights.
Your cousin, my lady, takes great exceptions to your ill
5   hours.

SIR TOBY BELCH
Why, let her except, before excepted.

MARIA
Ay, but you must confine yourself within the modest limits
of order.

SIR TOBY BELCH
Confine? I'll confine myself no finer than I am. These
10   clothes are good enough to drink in, and so be these boots
too. An they be not, let them hang themselves in their own
straps.

MARIA
That quaffing and drinking will undo you: I heard my lady
talk of it yesterday, and of a foolish knight that you brought
15   in one night here to be her wooer.

SIR TOBY BELCH
Who, Sir Andrew Aguecheek?

MARIA
Ay, he.

SIR TOBY BELCH
He's as tall a man as any 's in Illyria.

ACT 1, SCENE 3

SIR TOBY BELCH *and* MARIA *enter.*

SIR TOBY BELCH

What's wrong with my niece? Why is she reacting so strangely to her brother's death? Grief is bad for people's health.

MARIA

For God's sake, Sir Toby, you've got to come home earlier at night. My lady Olivia, your niece, disapproves of your late-night partying.

SIR TOBY BELCH

Well, she can get used to it.

MARIA

Yes, but you need to keep yourself within the limits of order and decency.

SIR TOBY BELCH

Keep myself? The only thing I'm keeping myself in is the clothes I'm wearing. They're good enough to drink in, and so are these boots. If they aren't, they can go hang themselves by their own laces!

MARIA

You're going to destroy yourself with all this drinking. Lady Olivia said so yesterday. She also mentioned some stupid knight you brought in one night as a possible husband for her.

SIR TOBY BELCH

Who, Sir Andrew Aguecheek?

MARIA

Yes, that's the one.

SIR TOBY BELCH

He's as tall as a man in Illyria.

"Tall" could be used as slang for "brave."

MARIA
What's that to the purpose?

SIR TOBY BELCH
20   Why, he has three thousand ducats a year.

MARIA
Ay, but he'll have but a year in all these ducats. He's a very
fool and a prodigal.

SIR TOBY BELCH
Fie, that you'll say so! He plays o' the viol-de-gamboys,
and speaks three or four languages word for word without
25   book, and hath all the good gifts of nature.

MARIA
He hath indeed, almost natural, for besides that he's a fool,
he's a great quarreler, and but that he hath the gift of a
coward to allay the gust he hath in quarreling, 'tis thought
among the prudent he would quickly have the gift of a grave.

SIR TOBY BELCH
30   By this hand, they are scoundrels and substractors that say
so of him. Who are they?

MARIA
They that add, moreover, he's drunk nightly in your
company.

SIR TOBY BELCH
With drinking healths to my niece. I'll drink to her as long
35   as there is a passage in my throat and drink in Illyria. He's
a coward and a coistrel that will not drink to my niece till his
brains turn o' th' toe like a parish top. What, wench!
Castiliano vulgo, for here comes Sir Andrew Agueface.

Enter SIR ANDREW

SIR ANDREW
Sir Toby Belch! How now, Sir Toby Belch!

SIR TOBY BELCH
40   Sweet Sir Andrew!

MARIA

What does his height have to do with anything?

SIR TOBY BELCH

Why, he has an income of three thousand ducats a year.

MARIA

I bet he'll spend his whole inheritance in a year. He's a fool and a spendthrift.

SIR TOBY BELCH

You shouldn't talk about him like that! He plays the violin and speaks three or four languages word for word without a dictionary. He has all of nature's best gifts.

MARIA

Right—he's a natural-born idiot. Besides being a fool, he's argumentative. If he didn't have the coward's gift for backing down from a fight, they say he'd be dead by now.

SIR TOBY BELCH

Anyone who says that is a lying piece of garbage. Who said that?

MARIA

The same people who say he gets drunk with you every night.

SIR TOBY BELCH

We only drink toasts to my niece. I'll drink to her as long as there's a hole in my throat and booze in Illyria. Anyone who refuses to drink to my niece until his brain spins around like a merry-go-round is scum. But speak of the devil, here comes Sir Andrew Agueface.

SIR ANDREW enters.

SIR ANDREW

Sir Toby Belch! How are you, Sir Toby Belch?

SIR TOBY BELCH

Sweet Sir Andrew!

SIR ANDREW
(to MARIA) Bless you, fair shrew.

MARIA
And you too, sir.

SIR TOBY BELCH
Accost, Sir Andrew, accost.

SIR ANDREW
What's that?

SIR TOBY BELCH
45   My niece's chambermaid.

SIR ANDREW
Good Mistress Accost, I desire better acquaintance.

MARIA
My name is Mary, sir.

SIR ANDREW
Good Mistress Mary Accost—

SIR TOBY BELCH
You mistake, knight. "Accost" is front her, board her, woo
50   her, assail her.

SIR ANDREW
By my troth, I would not undertake her in this company. Is
that the meaning of "accost"?

MARIA
Fare you well, gentlemen. (she starts to exit)

SIR TOBY BELCH
An thou let part so, Sir Andrew, would thou mightst never
55   draw sword again.

SIR ANDREW
An you part so, mistress, I would I might never draw sword
again. Fair lady, do you think you have fools in hand?

MARIA
Sir, I have not you by the hand.

SIR ANDREW

(to MARIA*)* And hello to you, my little wench.

MARIA

Hello, sir.

SIR TOBY BELCH

Chat her up, Sir Andrew. Chat her up.

SIR ANDREW

What?

SIR TOBY BELCH

This is my niece's maid.

SIR ANDREW

My dear Miss Chat-her-up, I look forward to getting to know you better.

MARIA

My name is Mary, sir.

SIR ANDREW

Miss Mary Chat-her-up—

SIR TOBY BELCH

No, you've got it wrong. When I said "chat her up," I wasn't saying her name. I was telling you to go after her, woo her, confront her.

SIR ANDREW

Good heavens, I'd never do that with people watching. Is that really what you meant?

MARIA

Goodbye, gentlemen. *(she starts to exit)*

SIR TOBY BELCH

She's leaving. If you let her go this easily, Sir Andrew, you don't deserve to ever use your sword again.

SIR ANDREW

If you leave like this, my dear, I won't ever use my sword again. I'm not just talking nonsense to you, I mean everything I say. Do you think you've got a couple of fools on your hands here?

MARIA

I'm not holding your hand, sir.

SIR ANDREW
Marry, but you shall have, and here's my hand.
(he offers her his hand)

MARIA
60   *(taking his hand)* Now, sir, thought is free. I pray you, bring
your hand to the buttery-bar and let it drink.

SIR ANDREW
Wherefore, sweetheart? What's your metaphor?

MARIA
It's dry, sir.

SIR ANDREW
Why, I think so. I am not such an ass, but I can keep my
65   hand dry. But what's your jest?

MARIA
A dry jest, sir.

SIR ANDREW
Are you full of them?

MARIA
Ay, sir, I have them at my fingers' ends. Marry, now I let go
your hand, I am barren.

Exit

SIR TOBY BELCH
70   O knight, thou lackest a cup of canary. When did I see thee
so put down?

SIR ANDREW
Never in your life, I think, unless you see canary put me
down. Methinks sometimes I have no more wit than a
Christian or an ordinary man has. But I am a great eater of
75   beef, and I believe that does harm to my wit.

SIR TOBY BELCH
No question.

SIR ANDREW

But you will. Here's my hand. *(he offers her his hand)*

MARIA

(taking his hand) A girl's got a right to her opinions. Take your hand to a bar and put a drink in it.

SIR ANDREW

Why, sweetheart? Is there a hidden meaning in this?

MARIA

You're not holding a glass. Your hand is dry, sir.

Maria implies that he's old and dried-up.

SIR ANDREW

Well, I hope so. I'm not such an idiot that I can't keep my hands dry. But I don't get it—what's the joke?

MARIA

Just a bit of my dry humor, sir.

SIR ANDREW

Are you always so funny?

MARIA

Yes, I've got a handful of jokes. But oops, when I let go of your hand, I let go of the biggest joke of all.

MARIA *exits.*

SIR TOBY BELCH

Sir, you need a drink. When has anyone ever put you down like that.

SIR ANDREW

Never. I've only been that far down when I've drunk myself under the table. Sometimes I think I'm no smarter than average. I eat a lot of red meat, and maybe that makes me stupid.

SIR TOBY BELCH

Absolutely.

SIR ANDREW
An I thought that, I'd forswear it. I'll ride home tomorrow, Sir Toby.

SIR TOBY BELCH
Pourquoi, my dear knight?

SIR ANDREW
80 What is "pourquoi"? Do, or not do? I would I had bestowed that time in the tongues that I have in fencing, dancing, and bear-baiting. O, had I but followed the arts!

SIR TOBY BELCH
Then hadst thou had an excellent head of hair.

SIR ANDREW
Why, would that have mended my hair?

SIR TOBY BELCH
85 Past question, for thou seest it will not curl by nature.

SIR ANDREW
But it becomes me well enough, does 't not?

SIR TOBY BELCH
Excellent. It hangs like flax on a distaff. And I hope to see a housewife take thee between her legs and spin it off.

SIR ANDREW
Faith, I'll home tomorrow, Sir Toby. Your niece will not be
90 seen. Or if she be, it's four to one she'll none of me. The count himself here hard by woos her.

SIR TOBY BELCH
She'll none o' the count. She'll not match above her degree, neither in estate, years, nor wit. I have heard her swear 't. Tut, there's life in 't, man.

SIR ANDREW

If I really believed that, I'd give up red meat totally. By the way, I'm going home tomorrow, Sir Toby.

SIR TOBY BELCH

Pourquoi, my friend?

Pourquoi *means "why" in French.*

SIR ANDREW

What does "*pourquoi*" mean? Does it mean I will or I won't? Oh, I wish I'd spent as much time learning languages as I spent on fencing, dancing, and bear-baiting! If only I'd taken school more seriously!

Bear-baiting, in which a bear was tied to a stake and attacked by dogs, was a popular entertainment in Shakespeare's time.

SIR TOBY BELCH

You'd have a great hairstyle if you had.

SIR ANDREW

Why, would that have fixed my hair?

SIR TOBY BELCH

Oh, no question—it won't style itself.

SIR ANDREW

But my hair looks good anyway, doesn't it?

SIR TOBY BELCH

It looks great. It hangs like an old worn-out mop. Some woman should give you syphilis so you go bald.

SIR ANDREW

Listen, I'm going home tomorrow, Sir Toby. Your niece is refusing to see anyone, and even if she saw me, ten to one she'd want nothing to do with me. That duke who lives nearby is courting her.

SIR TOBY BELCH

She's not interested in the duke. She doesn't want to marry anyone of higher social rank than her, or anyone richer, older, or smarter. I've heard her say that. So cheer up, there's still hope for you, man.

SIR ANDREW
95   I'll stay a month longer. I am a fellow o' th' strangest mind
        i' th' world. I delight in masques and revels sometimes
        altogether.

SIR TOBY BELCH
        Art thou good at these kickshawses, knight?

SIR ANDREW
        As any man in Illyria, whatsoever he be, under the degree
100   of my betters. And yet I will not compare with an old man.

SIR TOBY BELCH
        What is thy excellence in a galliard, knight?

SIR ANDREW
        Faith, I can cut a caper.

SIR TOBY BELCH
        And I can cut the mutton to 't.

SIR ANDREW
        And I think I have the back-trick simply as strong as any
105   man in Illyria.

SIR TOBY BELCH
        Wherefore are these things hid? Wherefore have these gifts
        a curtain before 'em? Are they like to take dust, like
        Mistress Mall's picture? Why dost thou not go to church in
        a galliard and come home in a coranto? My very walk
110   should be a jig. I would not so much as make water but in
        a sink-a-pace. What dost thou mean? Is it a world to hide
        virtues in? I did think, by the excellent constitution of thy
        leg, it was formed under the star of a galliard.

SIR ANDREW
        Ay, 'tis strong, and it does indifferent well in a dun-colored
115   stock. Shall we set about some revels?

SIR TOBY BELCH
        What shall we do else? Were we not born under Taurus?

SIR ANDREW

All right, I'll stay another month. Ah, I'm an odd kind of guy. Sometimes all I want to do is see plays and go out dancing.

SIR TOBY BELCH

Are you good at those kinds of things?

SIR ANDREW

Yes, as good as any man in Illyria, except for the ones who are better at it than I am. I'm not as good as someone who's been dancing for years.

SIR TOBY BELCH

How good are you at those fast dances?

SIR ANDREW

Believe me, I can cut a caper.

cut a caper = dance

SIR TOBY BELCH

And I can cut some meat to go with your capers.

caper = a condiment

SIR ANDREW

And I can do that fancy backward step as well as any man in Illyria.

SIR TOBY BELCH

Why do you hide these things? Why do you keep these talents behind a curtain? Are they likely to get dusty? Why don't you go off to church dancing one way, and come home dancing another way? If I had your talents, I'd be dancing a jig every time I walked down the street. I wouldn't even pee without dancing a waltz. What are you thinking? Is this the kind of world where we hide our accomplishments? You're a born dancer. Look how shapely your legs are.

SIR ANDREW

That's true. They're strong, and they look pretty good in brown tights. Should we throw a little dance party?

SIR TOBY BELCH

Why not? Weren't we both born under Taurus?

SIR ANDREW
Taurus! That's sides and heart.

SIR TOBY BELCH
No, sir, it is legs and thighs. Let me see the caper. (SIR
ANDREW *dances*) Ha, higher! Ha, ha, excellent!

Exeunt

SIR ANDREW

Taurus! That governs the torso and heart, doesn't it?

SIR TOBY BELCH

No, the legs and thighs. Let me see you dance. *(*SIR ANDREW *dances)* Ha, higher! Ha, ha, excellent!

They exit.

ACT 1, SCENE 4

Enter VALENTINE *and* VIOLA *in man's attire, as Cesario*

VALENTINE
If the duke continue these favors towards you, Cesario, you
are like to be much advanced. He hath known you but three
days, and already you are no stranger.

VIOLA
You either fear his humor or my negligence, that you call in
5 question the continuance of his love. Is he inconstant, sir, in
his favors?

VALENTINE
No, believe me.

VIOLA
I thank you. Here comes the count.

Enter ORSINO, CURIO, *and attendants*

ORSINO
Who saw Cesario, ho?

VIOLA
10 On your attendance, my lord, here.

ORSINO
(to VIOLA *and attendants)*
Stand you a while aloof. *(to* VIOLA*)* Cesario,
Thou know'st no less but all. I have unclasped
To thee the book even of my secret soul.
Therefore, good youth, address thy gait unto her;
15 Be not denied access, stand at her doors,
And tell them there thy fixed foot shall grow
Till thou have audience.

ACT 1, SCENE 4

VALENTINE enters with VIOLA, who is dressed as a young man named Cesario.

VALENTINE

If the Duke keeps treating you so well, Cesario, you'll go far. He's only known you for three days, but he's already treating you like a close friend.

VIOLA

When you wonder whether he'll keep treating me well, it makes me think his mood might change—or else I'll mess up somehow. Do his feelings toward people change suddenly?

VALENTINE

No, not at all.

VIOLA

Thanks for telling me. Here comes the Duke now.

ORSINO, CURIO, and attendants enter.

ORSINO

Has anyone seen Cesario?

VIOLA

I'm right here, my lord, at your service.

ORSINO

(to VIOLA and attendants) We'll need some privacy for a little while. *(to VIOLA)* Cesario, I want a word with you. You know everything about me. I've told you all the secrets of my soul. So please go to her house; if they don't let you in, plant yourself outside her door and tell them you won't leave until they let you see her.

VIOLA
                                        Sure, my noble lord,
        If she be so abandoned to her sorrow
        As it is spoke, she never will admit me.

ORSINO
20   Be clamorous, and leap all civil bounds,
        Rather than make unprofited return.

VIOLA
        Say I do speak with her, my lord, what then?

ORSINO
        O, then unfold the passion of my love,
        Surprise her with discourse of my dear faith:
25   It shall become thee well to act my woes;
        She will attend it better in thy youth
        Than in a nuncio's of more grave aspect.

VIOLA
        I think not so, my lord.

ORSINO
                                        Dear lad, believe it.
        For they shall yet belie thy happy years
30   That say thou art a man. Diana's lip
        Is not more smooth and rubious. Thy small pipe
        Is as the maiden's organ, shrill and sound,
        And all is semblative a woman's part.
        I know thy constellation is right apt
35   For this affair. *(to CURIO and attendants)*
                                Some four or five attend him.
        All, if you will, for I myself am best
        When least in company. *(to VIOLA)* Prosper well in this,
        And thou shalt live as freely as thy lord,
        To call his fortunes thine.

VIOLA
                                        I'll do my best
40   To woo your lady—*(aside)* Yet, a barful strife—
        Whoe'er I woo, myself would be his wife.

                                                Exeunt

VIOLA

But my lord, I'm sure that if she's as depressed as people say, she'll never let me in.

ORSINO

Be loud and obnoxious. Do whatever it takes, just get the job done.

VIOLA

Well, all right, let's say hypothetically that I do get a chance to speak with her, my lord. What do I do then?

ORSINO

Tell her how passionately I love her. Overwhelm her with examples of how faithful I am. The best thing would be to act out my feelings for her. She'll pay more attention to a young guy like you than to an older, more serious man.

VIOLA

I don't think so, my lord.

ORSINO

My boy, it's true. Anyone who says you're a man must not notice how young you are. Your lips are as smooth and red as the goddess Diana's. Your soft voice is like a young girl's, high and clear, and the rest of you is pretty feminine too. I know you're the right person for this job. *(to* CURIO *and attendants)* Four or five of you go along with him, or you can all go if you like. I'm most comfortable when I'm alone. *(to* VIOLA*)* If you succeed at this assignment, I'll reward you well. My whole fortune will be yours.

VIOLA

I'll do my best to make this lady love you.—*(to herself)* But what a tough task!—I have to go matchmaking for the man I want to marry myself!

They exit.

ACT 1, SCENE 5

Enter MARIA *and the* FOOL

MARIA

Nay, either tell me where thou hast been, or I will not open
my lips so wide as a bristle may enter in way of thy excuse.
My lady will hang thee for thy absence.

FOOL

Let her hang me. He that is well hanged in this world needs
5   to fear no colors.

MARIA

Make that good.

FOOL

He shall see none to fear.

MARIA

A good lenten answer. I can tell thee where that saying was
born, of "I fear no colors."

FOOL

10   Where, good Mistress Mary?

MARIA

In the wars. And that may you be bold to say in your
foolery.

FOOL

Well, God give them wisdom that have it. And those that
are fools, let them use their talents.

MARIA

15   Yet you will be hanged for being so long absent. Or to be
turned away, is not that as good as a hanging to you?

The fool, or jester,
makes his living
by amusing Olivia
and the members
of her household.

ACT 1, SCENE 5

MARIA *and the* FOOL *enter.*

MARIA

No. Either tell me where you've been, or I won't make
any excuses for you to Lady Olivia. Lady Olivia will
have you executed for not showing up.

FOOL

So let her execute me. Anyone who's executed doesn't
have to be afraid of anything he sees.

MARIA

How do you know?

FOOL

Well, he'll be dead, so he won't see anything.

MARIA

That's a lame answer. By the way, I know where you
get all your brave talk about not being afraid of anything.

FOOL

Where, good Miss Mary?

MARIA

From soldiers. But you'll never see the front lines. It's
easy for you to talk about bravery, working as a fool in
this palace.

FOOL

Well, we all have our special gifts. Some people are
born wise; those of us who were meant to be fools
should do what they do best.

MARIA

But still, she's going to kill you for being gone so long.
Or at least fire you. And wouldn't that be as bad for
you as being killed?

FOOL

> Many a good hanging prevents a bad marriage, and, for
> turning away, let summer bear it out.

MARIA

> You are resolute, then?

FOOL

20 Not so, neither, but I am resolved on two points.

MARIA

> That if one break, the other will hold. Or, if both break,
> your gaskins fall.

FOOL

> Apt, in good faith, very apt. Well, go thy way. If Sir Toby
> would leave drinking, thou wert as witty a piece of Eve's
25 flesh as any in Illyria.

MARIA

> Peace, you rogue, no more o' that. Here comes my lady.
> Make your excuse wisely, you were best.

Exit

FOOL

> *(aside)* Wit, an 't be thy will, put me into good fooling!
> Those wits, that think they have thee, do very oft prove
30 fools. And I, that am sure I lack thee, may pass for a wise
> man. For what says Quinapalus? "Better a witty fool, than
> a foolish wit."

Enter OLIVIA *with* MALVOLIO *with attendants*

> God bless thee, lady!

FOOL

Sometimes getting killed is a good way to avoid getting married. And as for being fired, it's summer, so it won't be that bad to be homeless.

MARIA

You've made up your mind, then?

FOOL

No, but I've made up my mind on two points.

MARIA

Ah yes, the two points where your suspenders are attached to your buttons. If one breaks, the other will hold, but if both points break, your pants will fall down.

FOOL

Clever, very clever. Well, go along now. You'd be the funniest person in Illyria . . . if Sir Toby ever stopped drinking.

MARIA

Shut up, you troublemaker, no more of that. Here comes my lady. If you know what's good for you, you'll think up some good excuse for being away so long.

MARIA *exits.*

FOOL

(to himself) Please, let me think of something funny to say now! Smart people who think they're witty often turn out to be fools, but I know I'm not witty, so I might pass for smart. What did that philosopher Quinapalus say? Ah yes, "A witty fool's better than a foolish wit."

Quinapalus is a made-up name →

OLIVIA *enters with* MALVOLIO *and attendants.*

Greetings to you, madam!

OLIVIA
Take the fool away.

FOOL
35   Do you not hear, fellows? Take away the lady.

OLIVIA
Go to, you're a dry fool. I'll no more of you. Besides, you
grow dishonest.

FOOL
Two faults, madonna, that drink and good counsel will
amend. For give the dry fool drink, then is the fool not dry.
40   Bid the dishonest man mend himself. If he mend, he is no
longer dishonest. If he cannot, let the botcher mend him.
Anything that's mended is but patched. Virtue that
transgresses is but patched with sin, and sin that amends
is but patched with virtue. If that this simple syllogism will
45   serve, so. If it will not, what remedy? As there is no
true cuckold but calamity, so beauty's a flower. The lady
bade take away the fool. Therefore, I say again, take
her away.

OLIVIA
Sir, I bade them take away you.

FOOL
50   Misprision in the highest degree! Lady, Cucullus non facit
monachum—that's as much to say as I wear not motley in
my brain. Good madonna, give me leave to prove you a
fool.

OLIVIA
Can you do it?

FOOL
55   Dexterously, good madonna.

OLIVIA

Get that fool out of here.

FOOL

Didn't you hear her, guys? Get the lady out of here.

OLIVIA

Oh, go away, you're a boring fool. I don't want to have anything to do with you anymore. Besides, you've gotten unreliable.

FOOL

Madam, those are two character flaws that a little booze and some common sense can fix. If you hand a drink to a sober fool, he won't be thirsty anymore. If you tell a bad man to mend his wicked ways, and he does, he won't be bad anymore. If he cannot, let the tailor mend him. Anything that's mended is only patched up. A good person who does something wrong is only patched up with sin. And a sinner who does something good is only patched up with goodness. If this logic works, that's great. If not, what can you do about it? Since the only real betrayed husband in the world is the one deserted by Lady Luck—because we're all married to her—beauty is a flower. The lady gave orders to take away the fool, so I'm telling you again, take her away.

OLIVIA

I told them to take *you* away.

FOOL

Oh, what a big mistake! Madam, you can't judge a book by its cover. I mean, I may look like a fool, but my mind's sharp. Please let me prove you're a fool.

OLIVIA

Can you do that?

FOOL

Easily, madam.

OLIVIA
> Make your proof.

FOOL
> I must catechise you for it, madonna. Good my mouse of
> virtue, answer me.

OLIVIA
> Well, sir, for want of other idleness, I'll bide your proof.

FOOL
60 Good madonna, why mournest thou?

OLIVIA
> Good fool, for my brother's death.

FOOL
> I think his soul is in hell, madonna.

OLIVIA
> I know his soul is in heaven, fool.

FOOL
> The more fool, madonna, to mourn for your brother's soul
65 being in heaven. Take away the fool, gentlemen.

OLIVIA
> What think you of this fool, Malvolio? Doth he not mend?

MALVOLIO
> Yes, and shall do till the pangs of death shake him.
> Infirmity, that decays the wise, doth ever make the better
> fool.

FOOL
70 God send you, sir, a speedy infirmity, for the better
> increasing your folly! Sir Toby will be sworn that I am no
> fox, but he will not pass his word for two pence that you are
> no fool.

OLIVIA
> How say you to that, Malvolio?

MALVOLIO
75. I marvel your ladyship takes delight in such a barren rascal.
> I saw him put down the other day with an ordinary fool that

NO FEAR SHAKESPEARE

OLIVIA

Then go ahead and prove it.

FOOL

I'll have to ask you some questions, madam. Please answer, my good little student.

OLIVIA

I'm listening to you only because I've got nothing better to do.

FOOL

My dear madam, why are you in mourning?

OLIVIA

My dear fool, because my brother died.

FOOL

I think his soul's in hell, my lady.

OLIVIA

I know his soul's in heaven, fool.

FOOL

Then you're a fool for being sad that your brother's soul is in heaven. Take away this fool, gentlemen.

OLIVIA

What do you think of this fool, Malvolio? Isn't he getting funnier?

MALVOLIO

Yes, and he'll keep getting funnier till he dies. Old age always makes people act funny—even wise people, but fools more than anybody.

FOOL

I hope you go senile soon, sir, so you can become a more foolish fool! Sir Toby would bet a fortune that I'm not smart, but he wouldn't bet two cents that you're not a fool.

OLIVIA

What do you say to that, Malvolio?

MALVOLIO

I'm surprised you enjoy the company of this stupid troublemaker. The other day I saw him defeated in a

has no more brain than a stone. Look you now, he's out of
his guard already. Unless you laugh and minister occasion
to him, he is gagged. I protest I take these wise men that
80   crow so at these set kind of fools no better than the fools'
zanies.

OLIVIA

Oh, you are sick of self-love, Malvolio, and taste with a
distempered appetite. To be generous, guiltless, and of free
disposition is to take those things for bird-bolts that you
85   deem cannon-bullets. There is no slander in an allowed
fool, though he do nothing but rail. Nor no railing in a
known discreet man, though he do nothing but reprove.

FOOL

Now Mercury endue thee with leasing, for thou speakest
well of fools!

Enter MARIA

MARIA

90   Madam, there is at the gate a young gentleman much
desires to speak with you.

OLIVIA

From the Count Orsino, is it?

MARIA

I know not, madam. 'Tis a fair young man, and well
attended.

OLIVIA

95   Who of my people hold him in delay?

MARIA

Sir Toby, madam, your kinsman.

OLIVIA

Fetch him off, I pray you. He speaks nothing but madman.
Fie on him!

battle of wits by an ordinary jester with no more brains than a rock. Look at him, he's at a loss for words already. Unless he's got somebody laughing at him, he can't think of anything to say. I swear, anyone smart who laughs at these courts jesters is nothing but a jester's apprentice.

OLIVIA

Malvolio, your vanity is damaging your good taste. If you were generous, innocent, and good-natured, you wouldn't get so upset by what the fool says. You'd think of his wisecracks as harmless little firecrackers, not hurtful bullets. A court jester isn't really criticizing people, even if he does nothing but make fun of them all day long. And a wise person doesn't make fun of people, even if all he does is criticize them.

FOOL

You speak so highly of fools! I hope the god of deception rewards you by making you a wonderful liar.

MARIA *enters.*

MARIA

Madam, there's a young gentleman at the gate who really wants to speak to you.

OLIVIA

Was he sent by Count Orsino?

MARIA

I don't know, madam. He's a good-looking young man, and there are a lot of people with him.

OLIVIA

Who's talking to him now?

MARIA

Sir Toby, madam, you're relative.

OLIVIA

Send Toby away, please. He talks nothing but nonsense.

Exit MARIA

Go you, Malvolio. If it be a suit from the count, I am sick,
100   or not at home. What you will, to dismiss it.

Exit MALVOLIO

Now you see, sir, how your fooling grows old, and people
dislike it.

FOOL

Thou hast spoke for us, madonna, as if thy eldest son
should be a fool, whose skull Jove cram with brains, for—
105   here he comes—one of thy kin has a most weak *pia mater*.

Enter SIR TOBY BELCH

OLIVIA

By mine honor, half-drunk. What is he at the gate, cousin?

SIR TOBY BELCH

A gentleman.

OLIVIA

A gentleman? What gentleman?

SIR TOBY BELCH

'Tis a gentleman here—a plague o' these pickle herring!
110   How now, sot!

FOOL

Good Sir Toby!

OLIVIA

Cousin, cousin, how have you come so early by this
lethargy?

MARIA *exits.*

Go out and talk to this visitor, Malvolio. If he's got a message from the count, tell him I'm sick, or not home. Tell him anything you want, as long as you make him go away.

MALVOLIO *exits.*

Now you see how your fooling gets boring, and people don't like it.

FOOL

Madam, you've spoken so highly of us fools, you'd think your oldest son was going into that line of work. I hope God crams his skull full of brains, because here comes one of your relatives who's pretty weak in the head.

SIR TOBY BELCH *enters.*

OLIVIA

I swear, he's half drunk already. Who's that at the gate, uncle?

SIR TOBY BELCH

A gentleman.

OLIVIA

A gentleman? What gentleman?

SIR TOBY BELCH

There's some gentleman out there.—*(belching)* Damn these pickled herring! They upset my stomach. How's it going, fool?

FOOL

Good Sir Toby!

OLIVIA

Uncle, uncle, how are you already so brain-dead so early in the day?

SIR TOBY BELCH
Lechery! I defy lechery. There's one at the gate.

OLIVIA
115   Ay, marry, what is he?

SIR TOBY BELCH
Let him be the devil, an he will, I care not. Give me faith, say I. Well, it's all one.

Exit

OLIVIA
What's a drunken man like, fool?

FOOL
Like a drowned man, a fool and a madman. One draught
120   above heat makes him a fool, the second mads him, and a third drowns him.

OLIVIA
Go thou and seek the crowner, and let him sit o' my coz. For he's in the third degree of drink, he's drowned. Go look after him.

FOOL
125   He is but mad yet, madonna, and the fool shall look to the madman.

Exit

Enter **MALVOLIO**

MALVOLIO
Madam, yond young fellow swears he will speak with you.
I told him you were sick. He takes on him to understand so much, and therefore comes to speak with you. I told him
130   you were asleep. He seems to have a foreknowledge of that too, and therefore comes to speak with you. What is to be said to him, lady? He's fortified against any denial.

SIR TOBY BELCH

> Brain-dead! Nonsense. I defy brain-death! I told you, someone's at the gate.

OLIVIA

> Yes, but who is he?

SIR TOBY BELCH

> Let him be the devil if he wants to, I don't care. God will protect me. What do I care who it is?

> *SIR TOBY BELCH exits.*

OLIVIA

> Tell me what a drunk is like, fool.

FOOL

> He's a fool, a madman, and a drowned man. The first drink makes him a fool, the second makes him crazy, and the third drowns him.

OLIVIA

> Go find the coroner and tell him to perform an inquest on my uncle, because he's in the third degree of drunkenness—he's drowned. Go take care of him.

FOOL

> He's still only in the crazy phase. The fool will go take care of the madman.

> *The FOOL exits.*

MALVOLIO enters.

MALVOLIO

> Madam, that young man out there says he's got to speak to you. I told him you were sick. He claimed he knew that, and that's why he's come to speak with you. I told him you were asleep. He claimed to know that already too, and said that's the reason he's come to speak with you. What can I say to him, lady? He's got an answer for everything.

OLIVIA
Tell him he shall not speak with me.

MALVOLIO
Has been told so, and he says he'll stand at your door like a
135   sheriff's post, and be the supporter to a bench, but he'll
speak with you.

OLIVIA
What kind o' man is he?

MALVOLIO
Why, of mankind.

OLIVIA
What manner of man?

MALVOLIO
140   Of very ill manner. He'll speak with you, will you or no.

OLIVIA
Of what personage and years is he?

MALVOLIO
Not yet old enough for a man, nor young enough for a boy,
as a squash is before 'tis a peascod, or a codling when 'tis
almost an apple. 'Tis with him in standing water, between
145   boy and man. He is very well-favored, and he speaks very
shrewishly. One would think his mother's milk were scarce
out of him.

OLIVIA
Let him approach. Call in my gentlewoman.

MALVOLIO
Gentlewoman, my lady calls.

Exit

Enter MARIA

OLIVIA
150   Give me my veil. Come, throw it o'er my face. *(OLIVIA puts
on a veil)* We'll once more hear Orsino's embassy.

Enter VIOLA, *with attendants*

OLIVIA

Tell him he's not going to speak with me.

MALVOLIO

I told him that. He says he'll stand at your door like a signpost or a bench until he speaks with you.

OLIVIA

What kind of man is he?

MALVOLIO

Just a man, like any other.

OLIVIA

But what's he like?

MALVOLIO

He's very rude. He insists he'll speak with you whether you want him to or not.

OLIVIA

What does he look like? How old is he?

MALVOLIO

Not old enough to be a man, but not young enough to be a boy. He's like a bud before it becomes a pea pod, or like a little green apple before it gets big and ripe. He's somewhere between boy and man. He's very handsome and speaks well, but he's very young. He looks like he just recently stopped breastfeeding.

OLIVIA

Show him in. Call in my maid.

MALVOLIO

Maria, our lady wants you.

MALVOLIO exits.

MARIA enters.

OLIVIA

Give me my veil. Come, put it over my face. *(OLIVIA puts on her veil)* We're going to hear Orsino's pleas again.

VIOLA enters, dressed as CESARIO, with attendants.

VIOLA
> The honorable lady of the house, which is she?

OLIVIA
> Speak to me. I shall answer for her. Your will?

VIOLA
> Most radiant, exquisite and unmatchable beauty—I pray
155 you, tell me if this be the lady of the house, for I never saw
> her. I would be loath to cast away my speech, for besides
> that it is excellently well penned, I have taken great pains to
> con it. Good beauties, let me sustain no scorn. I am very
> comptible, even to the least sinister usage.

OLIVIA
160 Whence came you, sir?

VIOLA
> I can say little more than I have studied, and that question's
> out of my part. Good gentle one, give me modest assurance
> if you be the lady of the house, that I may proceed in my
> speech.

OLIVIA
165 Are you a comedian?

VIOLA
> No, my profound heart. And yet, by the very fangs of
> malice I swear, I am not that I play. Are you the lady of the
> house?

OLIVIA
> If I do not usurp myself, I am.

VIOLA
170 Most certain, if you are she, you do usurp yourself, for what
> is yours to bestow is not yours to reserve. But this is from
> my commission. I will on with my speech in your praise and
> then show you the heart of my message.

VIOLA

Which one of you is the lady of the house?

OLIVIA

You can speak to me. I represent her. What do you want?

VIOLA

What stunning, exquisite, and unmatchable beauty—but please, tell me if you're the lady of the house, because I've never seen her. I'd hate to waste my speech on the wrong person, because it's very well written and I spent a lot of time and energy memorizing it. Beautiful ladies, please don't treat me badly. I'm very sensitive, and even the smallest bit of rudeness hurts my feelings.

OLIVIA

Where do you come from, sir?

VIOLA

I'm sorry, but I memorized what I'm supposed to say here today, and that question isn't part of the speech I learned. Please, my lady, just confirm that you're the lady of the house so I can get on with my speech.

OLIVIA

Are you an actor?

VIOLA

No, madam. But I swear I'm not the person I'm playing. Are you the lady of the house?

OLIVIA

I am, unless I somehow stole this role.

VIOLA

If you're the lady of the house, then it's true you're stealing your role, because what's yours to give away is not yours to keep for yourself. But that's not part of what I'm supposed to say. I'll go on with my speech praising you, and then I'll get to the point.

OLIVIA

Come to what is important in 't. I forgive you the praise.

VIOLA

175   Alas, I took great pains to study it, and 'tis poetical.

OLIVIA

It is the more like to be feigned. I pray you, keep it in. I
heard you were saucy at my gates and allowed your
approach rather to wonder at you than to hear you. If you
be not mad, be gone. If you have reason, be brief. 'Tis not
180   that time of moon with me to make one in so skipping a
dialogue.

MARIA

Will you hoist sail, sir? Here lies your way.

VIOLA

No, good swabber, I am to hull here a little longer. Some
mollification for your giant, sweet lady.

OLIVIA

185   Tell me your mind.

VIOLA

I am a messenger.

OLIVIA

Sure, you have some hideous matter to deliver, when the
courtesy of it is so fearful. Speak your office.

VIOLA

It alone concerns your ear. I bring no overture of war, no
190   taxation of homage. I hold the olive in my hand. My words
are as full of peace as matter.

OLIVIA

Yet you began rudely. What are you? What would you?

OLIVIA

Get to the point now. I'll let you get away with skipping the praise.

VIOLA

That's too bad, because I spent a long time memorizing it, and it's poetic.

OLIVIA

That means it's more likely to be fake. Please, keep it to yourself. I heard you were rude when you were standing outside my gate, and that's the only reason I let you in. I was curious. But I don't necessarily want to listen to you. If you're just insane, then get out of here. If you're in your right mind, get to the point. I've got no patience for lunacy at the moment, and I don't want to waste my time on ridiculous conversations.

MARIA

Ready to set sail, sir? The door's right here.

VIOLA

No, this boat's docking here a bit longer, little sailor.—My lady, would you mind asking your giant here to back off a bit?

OLIVIA

Tell me what you want.

VIOLA

I have a message to deliver.

OLIVIA

It must be a message about something horrible, since you deliver it so rudely. Tell me what it's about.

VIOLA

It's about you. I'm not bringing any declarations of war or demands for cash. I'm coming in peace.

OLIVIA

But you began so rudely. Who are you? What do you want?

VIOLA

The rudeness that hath appeared in me have I learned from
my entertainment. What I am and what I would are as
195   secret as maidenhead. To your ears, divinity. To any
other's, profanation.

OLIVIA

Give us the place alone. We will hear this divinity.

Exeunt MARIA *and attendants*

Now, sir, what is your text?

VIOLA

Most sweet lady—

OLIVIA

200   A comfortable doctrine, and much may be said of it. Where
lies your text?

VIOLA

In Orsino's bosom.

OLIVIA

In his bosom? In what chapter of his bosom?

VIOLA

To answer by the method, in the first of his heart.

OLIVIA

205   Oh, I have read it. It is heresy. Have you no more to say?

VIOLA

Good madam, let me see your face.

OLIVIA

Have you any commission from your lord to negotiate with
my face? You are now out of your text. But we will draw the
curtain and show you the picture. Look you, sir, such a one
210   I was this present. Is 't not well done?

VIOLA

If I seemed rude, it's because of how badly I was treated when I got here. Who I am and what I want are a secret. You're the only one I can share the secret with. It's sacred, just for you. It's not for anyone else to hear.

OLIVIA

Everyone, please leave us alone for a moment. I've got a "sacred" secret to hear.

MARIA and attendants exit.

Now, sir, what's this holy secret you wanted to tell me?

VIOLA

Most sweet lady—

OLIVIA

Oh, "sweet"! It sounds like a nice and gentle kind of faith. Where's the passage of holy scripture that you're basing your sermon on?

VIOLA

In Orsino's heart.

OLIVIA

In his heart? In what chapter and verse of his heart?

VIOLA

The table of contents says it's in the first chapter of his heart.

OLIVIA

Oh, I've read that. That's not holy, it's heresy. Do you have anything else to say?

VIOLA

Madam, please let me see your face.

OLIVIA

Has your lord given you any orders to negotiate with my face? I don't think so. You're overstepping your bounds now. But I'll open the curtain and let you see the picture. Look, sir, this is a portrait of me as I am at this particular moment. It's pretty well done, isn't it?

OLIVIA *removes her veil*

VIOLA

Excellently done, if God did all.

OLIVIA

'Tis in grain, sir. 'Twill endure wind and weather.

VIOLA

'Tis beauty truly blent, whose red and white
215   Nature's own sweet and cunning hand laid on.
Lady, you are the cruel'st she alive
If you will lead these graces to the grave
And leave the world no copy.

OLIVIA

O, sir, I will not be so hard-hearted. I will give out divers
220   schedules of my beauty. It shall be inventoried, and every
particle and utensil labeled to my will: as, item, two lips
indifferent red; item, two grey eyes, with lids to them; item,
one neck, one chin, and so forth. Were you sent hither to
praise me?

VIOLA

225   I see you what you are, you are too proud.
But, if you were the devil, you are fair.
My lord and master loves you. Oh, such love
Could be but recompensed though you were crowned
The nonpareil of beauty.

OLIVIA

                        How does he love me?

VIOLA

230   With adorations, fertile tears,
With groans that thunder love, with sighs of fire.

OLIVIA

Your lord does know my mind. I cannot love him.
Yet I suppose him virtuous, know him noble,
Of great estate, of fresh and stainless youth.

OLIVIA *takes off her veil.*

VIOLA

It was done excellently, if it's all-natural, the way God made it.

OLIVIA

Oh, it's all-natural, sir. Wind and rain can't wash it off.

VIOLA

That's true beauty. Mother Nature herself painted your skin so white and your lips so red. My lady, you'd be the cruelest woman alive if you let your beauty die with you, with no children to inherit your good looks for future generations to enjoy.

OLIVIA

Oh, I'd never be that cruel. I'll definitely do as you say and leave my beauty for the rest of the world to enjoy. I'll write out a detailed inventory of my beauty and label every part. For example—*item*: two lips, ordinary red. *Item*: two gray eyes, with lids on them. *Item*: one neck, one chin, and so on. Anyway, were you sent here just to tell me I'm beautiful?

VIOLA

I see what you're like. You're proud. But you'd still be gorgeous even if you were as proud as the devil. My lord loves you. You should return a love as deep as his, even if you're the most beautiful woman in the world.

OLIVIA

How does he love me?

VIOLA

He adores you. He cries and groans and sighs.

OLIVIA

Your lord knows what I think. I can't love him. I'm sure he's a very nice man. I know he's noble, rich, young, and with a fine reputation. People say he's generous, well educated, and brave, and he's very attrac-

235   In voices well divulged, free, learned, and valiant;
        And in dimension and the shape of nature
        A gracious person. But yet I cannot love him;
        He might have took his answer long ago.

VIOLA

        If I did love you in my master's flame,
240   With such a suffering, such a deadly life,
        In your denial I would find no sense;
        I would not understand it.

OLIVIA

                                    Why, what would you?

VIOLA

        Make me a willow cabin at your gate
        And call upon my soul within the house.
245   Write loyal cantons of contemned love
        And sing them loud even in the dead of night.
        Halloo your name to the reverberate hills
        And make the babbling gossip of the air
        Cry out "Olivia!" Oh, you should not rest
250   Between the elements of air and earth,
        But you should pity me.

OLIVIA

                                    You might do much.
        What is your parentage?

VIOLA

        Above my fortunes, yet my state is well.
        I am a gentleman.

OLIVIA

                            Get you to your lord.
255   I cannot love him. Let him send no more—
        Unless perchance you come to me again
        To tell me how he takes it. Fare you well.
        I thank you for your pains. Spend this for me.

        OLIVIA *offers* VIOLA *money*

tive. But I just can't love him. He should have resigned himself to that a long time ago.

VIOLA

If I loved you as passionately as my master does, and suffered like he does, your rejection would make no sense to me. I wouldn't understand it.

OLIVIA

What would you do about it?

VIOLA

I'd build myself a sad little cabin near your house, where my soul's imprisoned. From that cabin I'd call out to my soul. I'd write sad songs about unrequited love and sing them loudly in the middle of the night. I'd shout your name to the hills and make the air echo with your name, "Olivia!" Oh, you wouldn't be able to go anywhere without feeling sorry for me.

OLIVIA

Not bad; you might accomplish something. Who are your parents?

VIOLA

I was born to a higher position than I've got now. But I'm still fairly high-ranking. I'm a gentleman.

OLIVIA

Go back to your lord. I can't love him. Tell him not to send any more messengers—unless you feel like coming back to tell me how he took the bad news. Goodbye. Thanks for your trouble. Here's some money for you.

OLIVIA *offers* VIOLA *money.*

VIOLA

> I am no fee'd post, lady. Keep your purse.
260   My master, not myself, lacks recompense.
> Love make his heart of flint that you shall love,
> And let your fervor, like my master's, be
> Placed in contempt. Farewell, fair cruelty.

Exit

OLIVIA

> "What is your parentage?"
265   "Above my fortunes, yet my state is well.
> I am a gentleman." I'll be sworn thou art;
> Thy tongue, thy face, thy limbs, actions, and spirit,
> Do give thee fivefold blazon. Not too fast! Soft, soft!
> Unless the master were the man. How now?
270   Even so quickly may one catch the plague?
> Methinks I feel this youth's perfections
> With an invisible and subtle stealth
> To creep in at mine eyes. Well, let it be.—
> What ho, Malvolio!

Enter **MALVOLIO**

MALVOLIO

>   Here, madam, at your service.

OLIVIA

275   Run after that same peevish messenger,
> The county's man. He left this ring behind him,
> Would I or not. Tell him I'll none of it.

OLIVIA hands him a ring

> Desire him not to flatter with his lord,
> Nor hold him up with hopes. I am not for him.
280   If that the youth will come this way tomorrow,
> I'll give him reasons for 't. Hie thee, Malvolio.

VIOLA

I'm not a paid messenger, my lady. Keep your money. It's my master who's not getting the reward he deserves, not me. I hope you fall in love with a man whose heart is hard as a rock and who treats your love like a big joke, just like you've done. Goodbye, you beautiful, cruel woman.

VIOLA exits.

OLIVIA

"Who are your parents?" "I was born to a higher position than I've got now. But I'm still fairly high-ranking. I'm a gentleman." Yes, I'm sure you are. Your way of talking, your face, your body, your behavior, and your sensitive soul all prove you're a gentleman. Ah, no. Calm down, calm down. If only his lord were more like him. How strange I'm feeling! Can someone fall in love this quickly? I can feel this young man's perfection creeping in through my eyes like some kind of disease, slowly and invisibly. Oh, well.—Malvolio! Come here!

MALVOLIO enters.

MALVOLIO

At your service, madam.

OLIVIA

Run after that obnoxious messenger, the duke's servant. He insisted on leaving this ring with me whether I wanted it or not. Tell him I want nothing to do with it. *(she hands him a ring)* Ask him not to encourage Orsino or to get his hopes up. I'm not for him. If that young man comes here again tomorrow, I'll tell him why. Hurry, Malvolio.

MALVOLIO
Madam, I will.

Exit

OLIVIA
I do I know not what and fear to find
Mine eye too great a flatterer for my mind.
285   Fate, show thy force. Ourselves we do not owe.
What is decreed must be, and be this so.

Exit

MALVOLIO

Madam, I will.

MALVOLIO exits.

OLIVIA

I don't know what I'm doing. I'm afraid I'm not using my head, and I'm falling for his good looks. Fate, do your work. We human beings don't control our own destinies. What is fated to happen must happen. So let it happen!

OLIVIA exits.

ACT TWO
SCENE 1

Enter ANTONIO *and* SEBASTIAN

ANTONIO
Will you stay no longer, nor will you not that I go with you?

SEBASTIAN
By your patience, no. My stars shine darkly over me. The
malignancy of my fate might perhaps distemper yours.
5 Therefore I shall crave of you your leave that I may bear my
evils alone. It were a bad recompense for your love to lay
any of them on you.

ANTONIO
Let me yet know of you whither you are bound.

SEBASTIAN
No, sooth, sir. My determinate voyage is mere
10 extravagancy. But I perceive in you so excellent a touch of
modesty that you will not extort from me what I am willing
to keep in. Therefore it charges me in manners the rather to
express myself. You must know of me then, Antonio, my
name is Sebastian, which I called Roderigo. My father was
15 that Sebastian of Messaline, whom I know you have heard
of. He left behind him myself and a sister, both born in an
hour. If the heavens had been pleased, would we had so
ended! But you, sir, altered that, for some hour before you
took me from the breach of the sea was my sister drowned.

ANTONIO
20 Alas the day!

ACT TWO

SCENE 1

ANTONIO *and* SEBASTIAN *enter.*

ANTONIO

You won't stay any longer? And you don't want me to come with you?

SEBASTIAN

No, I'd rather you stayed here. My luck is pretty bad right now, and it might rub off on you. So just let me say goodbye and face the bad stuff alone—otherwise I wouldn't be thanking you very well for all you've done for me.

ANTONIO

At least tell me where you're going.

SEBASTIAN

Honestly, I can't. I'm just wandering, with no particular destination. But I know you'd never force me to tell you things I don't want to, so I should be polite and tell you what I can. My name's Sebastian, though I've been calling myself Roderigo. My father was Sebastian of Messaline. I know you've heard of him. He's dead now. He left behind myself and my twin sister, who was born in the same hour as me. If God had been willing, I wish we had died in the same hour too! But you kept that from happening. An hour before you pulled me out of the breaking waves, my sister drowned.

ANTONIO

How tragic!

SEBASTIAN
A lady, sir, though it was said she much resembled me, was
yet of many accounted beautiful. But though I could not
with such estimable wonder overfar believe that, yet thus
far I will boldly publish her: she bore a mind that envy
25   could not but call fair. She is drowned already, sir, with salt
water, though I seem to drown her remembrance again
with more.

ANTONIO
Pardon me, sir, your bad entertainment.

SEBASTIAN
O good Antonio, forgive me your trouble.

ANTONIO
30   If you will not murder me for my love, let me be your
servant.

SEBASTIAN
If you will not undo what you have done—that is, kill him
whom you have recovered—desire it not. Fare you well at
once. My bosom is full of kindness, and I am yet so near the
35   manners of my mother, that upon the least occasion more
mine eyes will tell tales of me. I am bound to the Count
Orsino's court. Farewell.

Exit

ANTONIO
The gentleness of all the gods go with thee!
I have many enemies in Orsino's court,
40   Else would I very shortly see thee there.
But, come what may, I do adore thee so
That danger shall seem sport, and I will go.

Exit

SEBASTIAN

Although many people said she looked like me, she was considered beautiful. And though I can't believe everything people said about her beauty, I'll be so bold as to say she had a beautiful mind. Even those who were jealous of her would have to admit that. She's been drowned in salty sea water, and now my salty tears are about to drown her memory all over again.

ANTONIO

I'm sorry I wasn't a better host for you, sir.

SEBASTIAN

Oh, Antonio, I'm sorry I caused you so much trouble.

ANTONIO

I care about you a lot. Please let me be your servant so I can be with you. You'll be killing me if you don't.

SEBASTIAN

If you don't want to break my heart, then say goodbye to me right now. I like you very much. I'm really about to cry, just like my mother would do. I'm going to Count Orsino's court. Goodbye.

SEBASTIAN *exits.*

ANTONIO

I wish you all the best. If I didn't have so many enemies in Orsino's court, I'd go join you there. But who cares. I'm so crazy about you that danger doesn't bother me. I'll go anyway.

ANTONIO *exits.*

ACT 2, SCENE 2

Enter VIOLA, MALVOLIO *following*

MALVOLIO
Were not you even now with the Countess Olivia?

VIOLA
Even now, sir. On a moderate pace I have since arrived but hither.

MALVOLIO
She returns this ring to you, sir. You might have saved me
5   my pains to have taken it away yourself. She adds,
moreover, that you should put your lord into a desperate
assurance she will none of him. And one thing more, that
you be never so hardy to come again in his affairs, unless it
be to report your lord's taking of this. Receive it so.

VIOLA
10   She took the ring of me. I'll none of it.

MALVOLIO
Come, sir, you peevishly threw it to her, and her will is it
should be so returned. *(he throws down the ring)* If it be
worth stooping for, there it lies in your eye. If not, be it his
that finds it.

Exit

VIOLA
15   I left no ring with her. What means this lady?
Fortune forbid my outside have not charmed her!
She made good view of me, indeed so much
That sure methought her eyes had lost her tongue,
For she did speak in starts distractedly.
20   She loves me, sure! The cunning of her passion
Invites me in this churlish messenger.

ACT 2, SCENE 2

VIOLA *enters with* MALVOLIO *following.*

MALVOLIO

Excuse me, weren't you with Countess Olivia just now?

VIOLA

Yes, sir. I've only made it this far since I left her place, walking at a moderate pace.

MALVOLIO

She's sending this ring back to you, sir. You should've saved me some trouble and taken it away yourself. She wants you to make it very clear to your lord that she wants nothing to do with him, and that you should never come again on his behalf, unless you want to come back to tell her how he reacted to the bad news. Here, take the ring.

VIOLA

She took that ring from me. I won't take it back.

MALVOLIO

You threw it at her rudely, and she wants you to take it back. *(he throws down the ring)* If it's worth bending over to pick up, there it is on the ground, where you can see it. If not, whoever finds it can have it.

MALVOLIO *exits.*

VIOLA

I didn't give her any ring. What's she trying to say? I hope she doesn't have a crush on me! It's true she looked at me a lot, in fact, she looked at me so much that she seemed distracted, and couldn't really finish her sentences very well. Oh, I really think she loves me! She sent this rude messenger to tell me to come back, instead of coming herself, which would be

None of my lord's ring? Why, he sent her none.
I am the man. If it be so, as 'tis,
Poor lady, she were better love a dream.
25 Disguise, I see thou art a wickedness,
Wherein the pregnant enemy does much.
How easy is it for the proper false
In women's waxen hearts to set their forms!
Alas, our frailty is the cause, not we,
30 For such as we are made of, such we be.
How will this fadge? My master loves her dearly,
And I, poor monster, fond as much on him,
And she, mistaken, seems to dote on me.
What will become of this? As I am man,
35 My state is desperate for my master's love.
As I am woman, now, alas the day,
What thriftless sighs shall poor Olivia breathe!
O time, thou must untangle this, not I.
It is too hard a knot for me to untie!

Exit

indiscreet. She doesn't want Orsino's ring! Orsino never sent her a ring. I'm the man she wants. If that's true, which it is, she might as well be in love with a dream, the poor lady. Now I understand why it's bad to wear disguises. Disguises help the devil do his work. It's so easy for a good-looking but deceitful man to make women fall in love with him. It's not our fault—we women are weak. We can't help what we're made of. Ah, how will this all turn out? My lord loves her, and. poor me, I love him just as much. And she's deluded enough to be in love with me. What can possibly fix this situation? I'm pretending to be a man, so my love for the Duke is hopeless. And since I'm a woman—too bad I'm a woman—Olivia's love for me is hopeless as well! Oh, only time can sort out this mess. I can't figure it out by myself!

VIOLA *exits.*

ACT 2, SCENE 3

Enter SIR TOBY BELCH *and* SIR ANDREW

SIR TOBY BELCH
Approach, Sir Andrew. Not to be abed after midnight is to
be up betimes, and *diluculo surgere,* thou know'st,—

SIR ANDREW
5   Nay, my troth, I know not. But I know to be up late is to be
up late.

SIR TOBY BELCH
A false conclusion. I hate it as an unfilled can. To be up after
midnight and to go to bed then, is early, so that to go to bed
after midnight is to go to bed betimes. Does not our life
10   consist of the four elements?

SIR ANDREW
Faith, so they say, but I think it rather consists of eating and
drinking.

SIR TOBY BELCH
Thou'rt a scholar. Let us therefore eat and drink. Marian,
I say! A stoup of wine!

Enter FOOL

SIR ANDREW
15   Here comes the fool, i' faith.

FOOL
How now, my hearts! Did you never see the picture of "We
Three"?

SIR TOBY BELCH
Welcome, ass. Now let's have a catch.

ACT 2, SCENE 3

SIR TOBY BELCH *and* SIR ANDREW *enter.*

SIR TOBY BELCH
Come on, Sir Andrew. If we're still awake after midnight, then we're up early in the morning. And the doctors say it's healthy to get up early—

SIR ANDREW
I don't know what the doctors say. All I know is that staying up late is staying up late.

SIR TOBY BELCH
A false conclusion. I hate your logic as much as I hate an empty drinking cup. Staying up after midnight means that you go to bed after midnight, in the wee hours of the morning, which is early. So it's like going to bed early. Isn't everybody made up of the four elements—earth, water, fire, and air?

SIR ANDREW
That's what they say, but I think life consists of food and booze.

SIR TOBY BELCH
You're a smart guy. So we should eat and drink. Maria! Bring us some wine!

The FOOL *enters.*

SIR ANDREW
Look, here comes the fool.

FOOL
Hello, my friends! What a pretty picture, three fools all together.

SIR TOBY BELCH
Hello, you idiot. Sing us a song.

SIR ANDREW

By my troth, the fool has an excellent breast. I had rather
20   than forty shillings I had such a leg, and so sweet a breath
to sing, as the fool has.—*(to the* FOOL*)* In sooth, thou wast
in very gracious fooling last night when thou spokest of
Pigrogromitus, of the Vapians passing the equinoctial of
Queubus. 'Twas very good, i' faith. I sent thee sixpence for
25   thy leman. Hadst it?

FOOL

I did impeticos thy gratillity, for Malvolio's nose is no
whipstock. My lady has a white hand, and the Myrmidons
are no bottle-ale houses.

SIR ANDREW

Excellent! Why, this is the best fooling when all is done.
30   Now, a song.

SIR TOBY BELCH

(giving money to the FOOL*)*
Come on. There is sixpence for you. Let's have a song.

SIR ANDREW

(giving money to the FOOL*)*
There's a testril of me too. If one knight give a—

FOOL

Would you have a love song or a song of good life?

SIR TOBY BELCH

A love song, a love song.

SIR ANDREW

35   Ay, ay. I care not for good life.

FOOL

(sings)
        O mistress mine, where are you roaming?
        O, stay and hear! Your true love's coming,
        That can sing both high and low:
        Trip no further, pretty sweeting.
40   *Journeys end in lovers meeting,*
        Every wise man's son doth know.

SIR ANDREW

> I swear, this fool has an excellent singing voice. I'd give forty shillings to have his nice legs and his beautiful voice. *(to the* FOOL*)* Fool, you were very funny last night talking that astrological nonsense about Pigrogromitus and the Vapians passing the equinox of Queubus. Very amusing. I sent you some money to spend on your girlfriend. Did you get it?

These are non-sense words that sound like astrology.

FOOL

> I gave your little present to my girlfriend because you can't get a grip on Malvolio's nose to whip your horse with it. My girlfriend has beautiful white hands, and great warriors aren't mom-and-pop diners, you know.

This is more nonsense to amuse Sir Andrew.

SIR ANDREW

> Ha, ha! I love it when you talk nonsense—that's what fools should do. Come on now, sing for us.

SIR TOBY BELCH

> *(giving the* FOOL *money)* Yes, come on. Here's sixpence for you. Let's hear a song.

SIR ANDREW

> *(giving the* FOOL *money)* Here's something from me too. If one knight gives—

FOOL

> Would you rather hear a love song or a song about the good life?

SIR TOBY BELCH

> A love song, a love song.

SIR ANDREW

> Yes, yes. I'm not interested in being good.

FOOL

> *(he sings)*
> Oh my lover, where are you roaming? Stay and listen! Your true love's coming, the one who can sing both high and low: Don't roam any further, pretty darling. Your journey ends when you meet a lover, as every wise man's son knows.

SIR ANDREW
Excellent good, i' faith.

SIR TOBY BELCH
Good, good.

FOOL
(sings)

> *What is love? 'Tis not hereafter.*
45 > *Present mirth hath present laughter.*
> *What's to come is still unsure.*
> *In delay there lies no plenty.*
> *Then come kiss me, sweet and twenty.*
> *Youth's a stuff will not endure.*

SIR ANDREW
50 A mellifluous voice, as I am true knight.

SIR TOBY BELCH
A contagious breath.

SIR ANDREW
Very sweet and contagious, i' faith.

SIR TOBY BELCH
To hear by the nose, it is dulcet in contagion. But shall we
make the welkin dance indeed? Shall we rouse the night owl
55 in a catch that will draw three souls out of one weaver? Shall
we do that?

SIR ANDREW
An you love me, let's do 't. I am dog at a catch.

FOOL
By 'r lady, sir, and some dogs will catch well.

SIR ANDREW
Most certain. Let our catch be "Thou Knave."

FOOL
60 "Hold thy peace, thou knave," knight? I shall be
constrained in 't to call thee knave, knight.

SIR ANDREW
That was excellent, really excellent.

SIR TOBY BELCH
Good, very good.

FOOL
(singing)
What is love? It isn't in the future. When you're having fun now, you're laughing right now. The future's unsure, and there's no reason to waste time. Come kiss me while you're twenty. You won't be young forever.

SIR ANDREW
A beautiful voice, I swear.

SIR TOBY BELCH
His breath stinks.

SIR ANDREW
Yes, it stinks very sweetly.

SIR TOBY BELCH
If we could listen to him with our noses, we would definitely say he stinks very sweetly. So what do you say, should we sing loud enough to shake the heavens? Should we sing a round to wake up the night owl? Should we do that?

SIR ANDREW
Let's go for it. I'm a very good singer, and can sing
dog = expert → rounds like a dog.

FOOL
Then you'll be good at catchy tunes. Dogs like to play catch.

SIR ANDREW
Absolutely. Let's dance to "You Jerk."

FOOL
You mean, "Shut up, you jerk"? That's the song where the singers call each other jerks, right? So I'll be forced to call you a jerk, Sir Andrew.

SIR ANDREW
'Tis not the first time I have constrained one to call me
"knave." Begin, Fool. It begins "Hold thy peace."

FOOL
I shall never begin if I hold my peace.

SIR ANDREW
65 Good, i' faith. Come, begin.

Catch sung

Enter **MARIA**

MARIA
What a caterwauling do you keep here! If my lady have not
called up her steward Malvolio and bid him turn you out of
doors, never trust me.

SIR TOBY BELCH
My lady's a Cataian. We are politicians, Malvolio's a Peg-
70 a-Ramsey, and (*sings*) Three merry men be we.—Am not I
consanguineous? Am I not of her blood? Tillyvally!
"Lady"! (*sings*) *There dwelt a man in Babylon, lady, lady!*

FOOL
Beshrew me, the knight's in admirable fooling.

SIR ANDREW
Ay, he does well enough if he be disposed, and so do I too.
75 He does it with a better grace, but I do it more natural.

SIR TOBY BELCH
(*sings*) *O' the twelfth day of December*—

MARIA
For the love o' God, peace!

Enter **MALVOLIO**

SIR ANDREW

It won't be the first time someone was forced to call me that. You start, Fool. It starts, "Shut up."

FOOL

I'll never be able to start if I shut up.

SIR ANDREW

That's true. But come on, start.

They sing.

MARIA *enters.*

MARIA

You're making a terrible racket out here! Lady Olivia told her servant Malvolio to kick you out of the house. I swear it's true.

SIR TOBY BELCH

Lady Olivia can go to China for all I care. We're very smart guys, and Malvolio's Little Bo Peep. *(he sings) We're just having some fun.*—Aren't I her relative, after all? Aren't we related? Fiddle-dee-dee, "Lady!" *(singing) There lived a man in Babylon, lady, lady!*

FOOL

Gosh, the knight's very good at acting like a fool.

SIR ANDREW

Yes, he's good at it when he's in the mood, and so am I. He's practiced more, but it comes more naturally to me.

SIR TOBY BELCH

(he sings) On the twelfth day of December—

MARIA

For God's sake, shut up!

MALVOLIO *enters.*

MALVOLIO

My masters, are you mad? Or what are you? Have you no wit, manners, nor honesty but to gabble like tinkers at this time of night? Do you make an alehouse of my lady's house, that you squeak out your coziers' catches without any mitigation or remorse of voice? Is there no respect of place, persons, nor time in you?

SIR TOBY BELCH

We did keep time, sir, in our catches. Sneck up!

MALVOLIO

Sir Toby, I must be round with you. My lady bade me tell you, that, though she harbors you as her kinsman, she's nothing allied to your disorders. If you can separate yourself and your misdemeanors, you are welcome to the house. If not, an it would please you to take leave of her, she is very willing to bid you farewell.

SIR TOBY BELCH

(sings) Farewell, dear heart, since I must needs be gone.

MARIA

Nay, good Sir Toby.

FOOL

(sings) His eyes do show his days are almost done.

MALVOLIO

Is 't even so?

SIR TOBY BELCH

(sings) But I will never die.

FOOL

(sings) Sir Toby, there you lie.

MALVOLIO

This is much credit to you.

MALVOLIO

Are you all crazy? What's wrong with you? Are you making all this noise at this time of night because you have no manners, or because you're just stupid? Are you trying to turn my mistress's house into a noisy bar? Is that why you're squealing out these ridiculous vulgar songs without lowering your voices at all? Don't you have any respect for anything?

SIR TOBY BELCH

We respected the beat of the song, sir. So shut up!

MALVOLIO

Sir Toby, I've got to be frank with you. My lady told me to tell you that while she lets you stay at her house because you're a relative, she doesn't approve of your behavior. If you can shape up, you're welcome to stay in the house. If you can't, and would prefer to leave, she's very willing to say goodbye to you.

SIR TOBY BELCH

(he sings) Goodnight, sweetheart, I'm going to leave you now.

In this line and the following lines, Sir Toby and the fool are singing variations on the lyrics of a popular song of the day.

MARIA

No, good Sir Toby.

FOOL

(singing) You can tell from his eyes that his life is almost over.

MALVOLIO

Is this how it's going to be?

SIR TOBY BELCH

(singing) But I will never die.

FOOL

(singing) Sir Toby, that's a lie.

MALVOLIO

This behavior really makes you look great.

SIR TOBY BELCH
(sings) Shall I bid him go?

FOOL
(sings) What an if you do?

100 **SIR TOBY BELCH**
(sings) Shall I bid him go, and spare not?

FOOL
(sings) O no, no, no, no, you dare not.

SIR TOBY BELCH
Out o' tune, sir. You lie. Art any more than a steward? Dost thou think, because thou art virtuous, there shall be no more cakes and ale?

105 **FOOL**
Yes, by Saint Anne, and ginger shall be hot i' the mouth too.

SIR TOBY BELCH
Thou'rt i' the right. Go, sir, rub your chain with crumbs. A stoup of wine, Maria!

MALVOLIO
Mistress Mary, if you prized my lady's favor at anything more than contempt, you would not give means for this
110 uncivil rule. She shall know of it, by this hand.

Exit

MARIA
Go shake your ears!

SIR ANDREW
'Twere as good a deed as to drink when a man's a-hungry, to challenge him the field and then to break promise with him and make a fool of him.

SIR TOBY BELCH
115 Do 't, knight. I'll write thee a challenge. Or I'll deliver thy indignation to him by word of mouth.

SIR TOBY BELCH

(singing) Should I tell him to go?

FOOL

(singing) What if y, ou do?

SIR TOBY BELCH

(singing) Should I tell him to go, and be harsh with him?

FOOL

(singing) Oh no, no, no, no, don't you dare.

SIR TOBY BELCH

That's out of tune, sir. You lie. *(to* MALVOLIO*)* You're nothing more than a servant here. Do you think that just because you're a goody two shoes, no one else can enjoy himself?

FOOL

They certainly will. They'll have double helpings, too.

SIR TOBY BELCH

You're right. *(to* MALVOLIO*)* Go polish your steward's chain, sir. Maria, bring us some wine!

MALVOLIO

Miss Mary, if you cared what Lady Olivia thinks about you at all, you wouldn't contribute to this rude behavior. I assure you, she'll find out about this.

MALVOLIO *exits.*

MARIA

Go and wiggle your ears!

SIR ANDREW

There's nothing I'd love more than to make a fool out of that guy somehow. I could challenge him to a duel and then not show up. That would do the trick.

SIR TOBY BELCH

Do that. I'll write a letter challenging him to a duel on your behalf. Or I'll deliver your insults to his face.

MARIA

Sweet Sir Toby, be patient for tonight. Since the youth of the count's was today with thy lady, she is much out of quiet. For Monsieur Malvolio, let me alone with him. If I
120   do not gull him into a nayword and make him a common recreation, do not think I have wit enough to lie straight in my bed. I know I can do it.

SIR TOBY BELCH

Possess us, possess us, tell us something of him.

MARIA

Marry, sir, sometimes he is a kind of puritan.

SIR ANDREW

125   O, if I thought that, I'd beat him like a dog!

SIR TOBY BELCH

What, for being a puritan? Thy exquisite reason, dear knight?

SIR ANDREW

I have no exquisite reason for 't, but I have reason good enough.

MARIA

The devil a puritan that he is, or anything constantly, but a
130   time-pleaser; an affectioned ass that cons state without book and utters it by great swarths; the best persuaded of himself, so crammed, as he thinks, with excellencies, that it is his grounds of faith that all that look on him love him. And on that vice in him will my revenge find notable cause
135   to work.

SIR TOBY BELCH

What wilt thou do?

MARIA

I will drop in his way some obscure epistles of love, wherein by the color of his beard, the shape of his leg, the manner of his gait, the expressure of his eye, forehead, and
140   complexion, he shall find himself most feelingly personated.

MARIA

> Dear Sir Toby, don't do anything rash tonight. Ever since the Duke's messenger visited Olivia, she's been upset. As for Monsieur Malvolio, let me take care of him. I'll make a big fool out of him, just trust me. I'll make him famous for his stupidity. Everyone will laugh at him. I know I can do it.

SIR TOBY BELCH

> Tell us something about him. Come on, tell us something.

MARIA

> Well, sometimes he acts like a goody two shoes.

SIR ANDREW

> Oh, I'll beat him up for that!

SIR TOBY BELCH

> You're going to beat him up for being good? And what's your brilliant reason for that, please?

SIR ANDREW

> I don't have any "brilliant" reason for it, but I have a good enough reason.

MARIA

> He isn't really that pure and good. He's just a conceited flatterer. He's a pretentious guy who aspires to speak and act like nobility. He's proud, and he thinks he's so stuffed full of wonderful qualities that everyone loves him. That's the weakness I'll use to get revenge on him.

SIR TOBY BELCH

> What are you going to do?

MARIA

> I'll drop some mysterious love letters in his path. He'll think they're addressed to him, because they'll describe the color of his beard, the shape of his legs, the way he walks, and the expression on his face. I can make my handwriting look just like Lady Olivia's: she

I can write very like my lady your niece: on a forgotten matter
we can hardly make distinction of our hands.

SIR TOBY BELCH
Excellent! I smell a device.

SIR ANDREW
I have 't in my nose too.

SIR TOBY BELCH
145   He shall think, by the letters that thou wilt drop, that they
come from my niece, and that she's in love with him.

MARIA
My purpose is, indeed, a horse of that color.

SIR ANDREW
And your horse now would make him an ass.

MARIA
Ass, I doubt not.

SIR ANDREW
150   Oh, 'twill be admirable!

MARIA
Sport royal, I warrant you. I know my physic will work with
him. I will plant you two, and let the fool make a third,
where he shall find the letter. Observe his construction of it.
For this night, to bed, and dream on the event. Farewell.

Exit

SIR TOBY BELCH
155   Good night, Penthesilea.

SIR ANDREW
Before me, she's a good wench.

SIR TOBY BELCH
She's a beagle, true-bred, and one that adores me. What o'
that?

SIR ANDREW
I was adored once too.

and I can't tell the difference between each other's handwriting.

SIR TOBY BELCH

Excellent! Sounds like you've got a good trick in mind.

SIR ANDREW

I like it too.

SIR TOBY BELCH

He'll think these letters are from Olivia and that she's in love with him.

MARIA

Yes, that's the idea.

SIR ANDREW

He's going to look like a total idiot.

MARIA

Absolutely, you idiot.

SIR ANDREW

This is going to be great!

MARIA

It's going to be fun, I promise. I know my medicine will work on him. I'll have you two hide—and the fool too—right where he'll find the letter. Watch his reaction. Meanwhile, let's go to bed and dream about this. Good night.

MARIA exits.

SIR TOBY BELCH

Good night, you amazing woman, you.

SIR ANDREW

She's a fine woman, all right.

SIR TOBY BELCH

She's a good little woman, and she adores me. What about it?

SIR ANDREW

Someone adored me once, too.

SIR TOBY BELCH
160   Let's to bed, knight. Thou hadst need send for more money.

SIR ANDREW
        If I cannot recover your niece, I am a foul way out.

SIR TOBY BELCH
        Send for money, knight. If thou hast her not i' the end, call
        me "Cut."

SIR ANDREW
        If I do not, never trust me, take it how you will.

SIR TOBY BELCH
165   Come, come, I'll go burn some sack. 'Tis too late to go to
        bed now. Come, knight. Come, knight.

                                                    Exeunt

NO FEAR SHAKESPEARE

SIR TOBY BELCH

Let's go to bed, knight. Tomorrow you need to get more money sent to you.

SIR ANDREW

If I can't persuade your niece to marry me, I'm going to be in some serious financial trouble.

SIR TOBY BELCH

Get your hands on some money and everything will be all right. I know you'll win over Olivia in the end.

SIR ANDREW

I know I will too, if it's the last thing I do.

SIR TOBY BELCH

Come on, I'll go warm up a nice glass of sherry for us. It's too late to go to bed now. Come on, my friend, come on.

They exit.

ACT 2, SCENE 4

Enter ORSINO, VIOLA, CURIO, *and others*

ORSINO
Give me some music. (*music plays*)
Now, good morrow, friends.—
Now, good Cesario, but that piece of song,
That old and antique song we heard last night.
5   Methought it did relieve my passion much,
More than light airs and recollected terms
Of these most brisk and giddy-paced times:
Come, but one verse.

CURIO
He is not here, so please your lordship, that should sing it.

ORSINO
10   Who was it?

CURIO
Feste, the jester, my lord, a fool that the lady Olivia's father
took much delight in. He is about the house.

ORSINO
Seek him out, and play the tune the while.

Exit CURIO. *Music plays*

(*to* VIOLA) Come hither, boy. If ever thou shalt love,
15   In the sweet pangs of it remember me;
For such as I am, all true lovers are,
Unstaid and skittish in all motions else
Save in the constant image of the creature
That is beloved. How dost thou like this tune?

VIOLA
20   It gives a very echo to the seat
Where Love is throned.

ACT 2, SCENE 4

ORSINO, VIOLA, CURIO, *and others enter.*

ORSINO

Play me some music. *(music plays)* Good morning, my friends.—Have them sing me that song again, Cesario, that old-fashioned song someone sang last night. It made me feel better and took my mind off my troubles much better than the silly songs they sing nowadays. Please, have them sing just one verse.

CURIO

Sir, the person who should sing that song isn't here.

ORSINO

Who was it?

CURIO

Feste, the jester, my lord. Olivia's father used to like him. He's somewhere else in the house.

ORSINO

Then go find him. Meanwhile, play the tune.

CURIO *exits. Music plays.*

(to VIOLA*)* Come here, boy. If you ever fall in love and feel the bittersweet pain it brings, think of me. Because the way I am now, moody and unable to focus on anything except the face of the woman I love, is exactly how all true lovers are. What do you think of this song?

VIOLA

It really makes you feel what a lover feels.

ORSINO
                    Thou dost speak masterly.
My life upon 't, young though thou art, thine eye
Hath stay'd upon some favor that it loves.
Hath it not, boy?

VIOLA
                    A little, by your favor.

ORSINO
25   What kind of woman is't?

VIOLA
                    Of your complexion.

ORSINO
She is not worth thee, then. What years, i' faith?

VIOLA
About your years, my lord.

ORSINO
Too old by heaven. Let still the woman take
An elder than herself. So wears she to him,
30   So sways she level in her husband's heart.
For, boy, however we do praise ourselves,
Our fancies are more giddy and unfirm,
More longing, wavering, sooner lost and worn,
Than women's are.

VIOLA
                    I think it well, my lord.

ORSINO
35   Then let thy love be younger than thyself,
Or thy affection cannot hold the bent.
For women are as roses, whose fair flower
Being once displayed, doth fall that very hour.

VIOLA
And so they are. Alas, that they are so,
40   To die even when they to perfection grow!

Enter CURIO *and* FOOL

ORSINO

You're absolutely right. I'd bet my life that, as young as you are, you've fallen in love with someone. Haven't you, boy?

VIOLA

A little bit.

ORSINO

What kind of woman is she?

VIOLA

She's a lot like you.

ORSINO

She's not good enough for you, then. How old is she?

VIOLA

About as old as you are, my lord.

ORSINO

That's definitely too old. A woman should always pick an older man. That way she'll adjust herself to what her husband wants, and the husband will be happy and faithful to her. Because however much we like to brag, boy, the truth is that we men change our minds a lot more than women do, and our desires come and go a lot faster than theirs.

VIOLA

I think you're right, sir.

ORSINO

So find someone younger to love, or you won't be able to maintain your feelings. Women are like roses: the moment their beauty is in full bloom, it's about to decay.

VIOLA

That's true. It's too bad their beauty fades right when it reaches perfection!

CURIO *and the* FOOL *enter.*

ORSINO
O, fellow, come, the song we had last night.—
Mark it, Cesario, it is old and plain;
The spinsters and the knitters in the sun
And the free maids that weave their thread with bones
45   Do use to chant it. It is silly sooth,
And dallies with the innocence of love,
Like the old age.

FOOL
                                   Are you ready, sir?

ORSINO
Ay; prithee, sing.

Music

FOOL
(sings)
                Come away, come away, death,
50   And in sad cypress let me be laid.
                Fly away, fly away breath,
                I am slain by a fair cruel maid.
                My shroud of white, stuck all with yew,
                O, prepare it!
55   My part of death, no one so true
                Did share it.
                Not a flower, not a flower sweet
                On my black coffin let there be strown.
                Not a friend, not a friend greet
60   My poor corpse, where my bones shall be thrown.
                A thousand thousand sighs to save,
                Lay me, O, where
                Sad true lover never find my grave,
                To weep there!

ORSINO
65   *(giving money)* There's for thy pains.

ORSINO

My friend, sing us the song you sang last night.—Listen to it carefully, Cesario, it's a simple old song. Spinners and knitters used to sing it while they sewed, and maidens used to sing it over their weaving. It tells the simple truth about innocent love, as it was in the good old days.

FOOL

Are you ready, sir?

ORSINO

Yes. Please, sing.

Music plays.

.

FOOL

(he sings)
> *Come on, let me die now*
> *And put my body in a dark coffin.*
> *I feel my breath leaving me.*
> *I've been killed by a beautiful girl.*
> *Prepare my shroud of white,*
> *Adorned with sprigs of yew-tree.*
> *I'm the most faithful person*
> *Who ever lived or died.*
> *Don't scatter sweet flowers*
> *On my black coffin.*
> *Don't let my friends*
> *See my poor corpse.*
> *I don't want to hear sad sighs,*
> *So bury me where no sad lovers*
> *can find my grave to weep over it!*

ORSINO

(giving the FOOL *money)* Here's some money for your trouble.

FOOL

No pains, sir. I take pleasure in singing, sir.

ORSINO

I'll pay thy pleasure then.

FOOL

Truly, sir, and pleasure will be paid, one time or another.

ORSINO

Give me now leave to leave thee.

FOOL

70   Now, the melancholy god protect thee, and the tailor make
        thy doublet of changeable taffeta, for thy mind is a very
        opal. I would have men of such constancy put to sea, that
        their business might be everything and their intent
        everywhere, for that's it that always makes a good voyage of
75   nothing. Farewell.

                                                        Exit

ORSINO

Let all the rest give place.

                                        CURIO *and attendants retire*

                                        Once more, Cesario,
        Get thee to yond same sovereign cruelty.
        Tell her my love, more noble than the world,
        Prizes not quantity of dirty lands;
80   The parts that fortune hath bestowed upon her,
        Tell her, I hold as giddily as fortune;
        But 'tis that miracle and queen of gems
        That nature pranks her in attracts my soul.

VIOLA

But if she cannot love you, sir?

FOOL

No trouble, sir. I like singing.

ORSINO

Then I'll pay you for doing what you like.

FOOL

Well, in that case, all right. We all pay for what we like sooner or later.

ORSINO

You may leave.

FOOL

I'll pray for the god of sadness to protect you, sir. And I hope your tailor will make you an outfit out of fabric that changes color, because your mind is like an opal that changes colors constantly. Men as wonderfully changeable as you are should all go drifting on the sea, where they can do whatever comes their way, and go wherever the current takes them. Those are the men whose trips are always successful. Goodbye.

The **FOOL** *exits.*

ORSINO

All the rest of you can leave too.

CURIO *and attendants retire.*

Cesario, go visit that cruel Olivia one more time. Tell her my love is purer than anything else in the whole world, and has nothing to do with her property. The wealth she's inherited isn't what makes me value her. It's her rich, jewel-like beauty that attracts me.

VIOLA

But if she can't love you, sir?

ORSINO

85   I cannot be so answer'd.

VIOLA

                                   Sooth, but you must.
          Say that some lady, as perhaps there is,
          Hath for your love a great a pang of heart
          As you have for Olivia. You cannot love her.
          You tell her so. Must she not then be answered?

ORSINO

90   There is no woman's sides
          Can bide the beating of so strong a passion
          As love doth give my heart. No woman's heart
          So big, to hold so much. They lack retention.
          Alas, their love may be called appetite,
95   No motion of the liver, but the palate,
          That suffer surfeit, cloyment, and revolt;
          But mine is all as hungry as the sea,
          And can digest as much. Make no compare
          Between that love a woman can bear me
100   And that I owe Olivia.

VIOLA

                                   Ay, but I know—

ORSINO

          What dost thou know?

VIOLA

          Too well what love women to men may owe.
          In faith, they are as true of heart as we.
          My father had a daughter loved a man
105   As it might be, perhaps, were I a woman,
          I should your lordship.

ORSINO

                                   And what's her history?

ORSINO

I refuse to accept that.

VIOLA

But you have to. Just imagine some lady might exist who loves you as powerfully and agonizingly as you love Olivia. But you can't love her, and you tell her so. Shouldn't she just accept that?

ORSINO

No woman is strong enough to put up with the kind of intense passion I feel. No woman's heart is big enough to hold all my love. Women don't feel love like that—love is as shallow as appetite for them. It has nothing to do with their hearts, just their sense of taste. They eat too much and get indigestion and nausea. But my love's different. It's as all-consuming and insatiable as the sea, and it can swallow as much as the sea can. Don't compare a woman's love for a man with my love for Olivia.

VIOLA

Yes, but I know—

ORSINO

What do you know?

VIOLA

I know a lot about the love women can feel for men. Actually, their hearts are as sensitive and loyal as ours are. My father had a daughter who loved a man in the same way that I might love you, if I were a woman.

ORSINO

And what's her story?

VIOLA

A blank, my lord. She never told her love,
But let concealment, like a worm i' the bud,
Feed on her damask cheek. She pined in thought,
110   And with a green and yellow melancholy
She sat like patience on a monument,
Smiling at grief. Was not this love indeed?
We men may say more, swear more, but indeed
Our shows are more than will, for still we prove
115   Much in our vows, but little in our love.

ORSINO

But died thy sister of her love, my boy?

VIOLA

I am all the daughters of my father's house,
And all the brothers too—and yet I know not.
Sir, shall I to this lady?

ORSINO

                              Ay, that's the theme.
120   To her in haste. Give her this jewel. Say
My love can give no place, bide no denay.
(he hands her a jewel)

                                        Exeunt

VIOLA

There was no story, my lord. She never told him she loved him. She kept her love bottled up inside her until it destroyed her, ruining her beauty. She pined away. She just sat waiting patiently, sadly, smiling despite her sadness. Her complexion turned greenish from depression. Doesn't that sound like true love? We men might talk more and promise more, but in fact we talk more than we really feel. We might be great at making vows, but our love isn't sincere.

ORSINO

But did your sister die of love?

VIOLA

I am the only daughter in my father's family, and all the brothers too—but I'm not completely sure about that. Anyway, sir, should I go see the lady?

ORSINO

Yes, go quickly and give her this jewel. Tell her my love won't go away and won't be denied. *(he hands her a jewel)*

They exit.

ACT 2, SCENE 5

Enter SIR TOBY BELCH, SIR ANDREW, *and* FABIAN

SIR TOBY BELCH
Come thy ways, Signior Fabian.

FABIAN
Nay, I'll come. If I lose a scruple of this sport, let me be
boiled to death with melancholy.

SIR TOBY BELCH
Wouldst thou not be glad to have the niggardly rascally
5   sheep-biter come by some notable shame?

FABIAN
I would exult, man. You know, he brought me out o' favor
with my lady about a bear-baiting here.

SIR TOBY BELCH
To anger him, we'll have the bear again, and we will fool
him black and blue. Shall we not, Sir Andrew?

SIR ANDREW
10   An we do not, it is pity of our lives.

SIR TOBY BELCH
Here comes the little villain.

Enter MARIA

How now, my metal of India?

MARIA
Get you all three into the boxtree. Malvolio's coming down
this walk. He has been yonder i' the sun practising behavior
15   to his own shadow this half hour. Observe him, for the love
of mockery, for I know this letter will make a contemplative
idiot of him. Close, in the name of jesting!

ACT 2, SCENE 5

SIR TOBY BELCH, SIR ANDREW, *and* FABIAN *enter.*

SIR TOBY BELCH
Come along with us, Signor Fabian.

FABIAN
I'm coming, don't worry. If I miss this, let me be boiled alive.

SIR TOBY BELCH
Won't you be glad to see that rascal dog humiliated?

FABIAN
I'll be thrilled. You know, he got me in trouble with the lady of the house once when I arranged a bear-baiting here.

SIR TOBY BELCH
We'll have another bear-baiting just to make him angry, and we'll mock him till he's black and blue. Won't we, Sir Andrew?

SIR ANDREW
If we don't, it'll be the biggest disappointment of our lives.

SIR TOBY BELCH
Here comes the little villain herself.

MARIA *enters.*

How are you, my golden girl?

MARIA
Hide behind the boxwood hedge, all three of you. Malvolio's coming down the path. He's been over there practicing how to act for the past half hour. Watch him carefully if you want to have some fun, guys. This letter's going to turn him into a starry-eyed idiot. Now hide, for God's sake!

They hide

Lie thou there (throwing down a letter), for here comes the
trout that must be caught with tickling.

Exit

Enter MALVOLIO

MALVOLIO
20   'Tis but fortune, all is fortune. Maria once told me she did
        affect me, and I have heard herself come thus near, that,
        should she fancy, it should be one of my complexion.
        Besides, she uses me with a more exalted respect than
        anyone else that follows her. What should I think on 't?

SIR TOBY BELCH
25   (*aside*) Here's an overweening rogue!

FABIAN
        (*aside*) O, peace! Contemplation makes a rare turkey-cock
        of him. How he jets under his advanced plumes!

SIR ANDREW
        (*aside*) 'Slight, I could so beat the rogue!

SIR TOBY BELCH
        (*aside*) Peace, I say.

MALVOLIO
30   To be Count Malvolio!

SIR TOBY BELCH
        (*aside*) Ah, rogue!

SIR ANDREW
        (*aside*) Pistol him, pistol him.

SIR TOBY BELCH
        (*aside*) Peace, peace!

They all hide.

Now, you lie there on the path. (**MARIA** *throws down a letter*) Here comes the fish that's going to gobble up our bait.

MARIA *exits.*

MALVOLIO *enters.*

MALVOLIO

It's all luck. Everything's luck. Maria once told me Olivia was fond of me. I've almost heard Olivia say that herself. She said if she were interested in someone, it would be someone who looked like me. Besides, she treats me more respectfully than the other servants. What's the obvious conclusion from that?

SIR TOBY BELCH

(whispering) What an egomaniac!

FABIAN

(whispering) Shh! When he's alone with his thoughts, he's even more like a haughty peacock. Watch him strut!

SIR ANDREW

(whispering) I swear, I'd like to beat the jerk so hard!

SIR TOBY BELCH

(whispering) Be quiet!

MALVOLIO

Just think, I could be Count Malvolio!

SIR TOBY BELCH

(whispering) Ah, what a jerk!

SIR ANDREW

(whispering) Shoot him, just shoot him.

SIR TOBY BELCH

(whispering) Shh, shh!

MALVOLIO
There is example for 't. The lady of the Strachy married the
35   yeoman of the wardrobe.

SIR ANDREW
(*aside*) Fie on him, Jezebel!

FABIAN
(*aside*) O, peace! Now he's deeply in. Look how
imagination blows him.

MALVOLIO
Having been three months married to her, sitting in my
40   state—

SIR TOBY BELCH
(*aside*) Oh, for a stone-bow, to hit him in the eye!

MALVOLIO
Calling my officers about me, in my branched velvet gown,
having come from a daybed, where I have left Olivia
sleeping—

SIR TOBY BELCH
45   (*aside*) Fire and brimstone!

FABIAN
(*aside*) O, peace, peace!

MALVOLIO
And then to have the humor of state, and after a demure
travel of regard, telling them I know my place as I would
they should do theirs, to ask for my kinsman Toby—

SIR TOBY BELCH
50   (*aside*) Bolts and shackles!

FABIAN
(*aside*) O peace, peace, peace! Now, now.

MALVOLIO

After all, it wouldn't be the first time that kind of thing has happened. Lady Strachy married her wardrobe manager.

SIR ANDREW

(whispering) Damn him, the arrogant fool!

FABIAN

(whispering) Shh! We've got him right where we want him. He's on a big ego trip.

MALVOLIO

Just think of me, having been married to her for three months, sitting around majestically—

SIR TOBY BELCH

(whispering) If only I had a slingshot so I could hit him in the eye!

MALVOLIO

Calling my servants together, wearing an embroidered robe, having just come from a couch where I've left Olivia sleeping—

SIR TOBY BELCH

(whispering) That does it!

FABIAN

(whispering) Oh, be quiet, be quiet!

MALVOLIO

Then I'd put on a lofty and exalted expression. I'd look around the room calmly, then tell them that I know my place, and I'd like them to know theirs. Then I'd tell them to go find my cousin Toby—

SIR TOBY BELCH

(whispering) That really does it!

FABIAN

(whispering) Oh, quiet, quiet! Please, please.

MALVOLIO
Seven of my people, with an obedient start, make out for
him. I frown the while, and perchance wind up watch, or
play with my—some rich jewel. Toby approaches, curtsies
55   there to me—

SIR TOBY BELCH
(*aside*) Shall this fellow live?

FABIAN
(*aside*) Though our silence be drawn from us with cars, yet
peace.

MALVOLIO
I extend my hand to him thus, quenching my familiar smile
60   with an austere regard of control—

SIR TOBY BELCH
(*aside*) And does not Toby take you a blow o' the lips then?

MALVOLIO
Saying, "Cousin Toby, my fortunes having cast me on your
niece give me this prerogative of speech—"

SIR TOBY BELCH
(*aside*) What, what?

MALVOLIO
65   "You must amend your drunkenness."

SIR TOBY BELCH
(*aside*) Out, scab!

FABIAN
(*aside*) Nay, patience, or we break the sinews of our plot.

MALVOLIO
"Besides, you waste the treasure of your time with a foolish
knight—"

SIR ANDREW
70   (*aside*) That's me, I warrant you.

MALVOLIO
"One Sir Andrew—"

MALVOLIO

> I'd send seven of my servants to go get him. While I waited, I'd frown impatiently, and perhaps wind my watch, or play with my—with some expensive piece of jewelry I happen to be wearing. Toby would approach me. He'd bow to me—

SIR TOBY BELCH

> (whispering) Are we going to let this guy live?

FABIAN

> (whispering) Yes, we have to be quiet, even if it's torture.

MALVOLIO

> I reach out my hand to him like this, giving him a stern look instead of my usual friendly smile—

SIR TOBY BELCH

> (whispering) And then doesn't Toby punch you in the mouth?

MALVOLIO

> And I'd say to him, "Cousin Toby, since I've been lucky enough to marry your niece, I have the right to say a few things to you—"

SIR TOBY BELCH

> (whispering) Oh yeah, like what?

MALVOLIO

> "You must stop being such a drunk."

SIR TOBY BELCH

> (whispering) Get out of here, you scab!

FABIAN

> (whispering) No, be quiet, or we'll screw up the joke.

MALVOLIO

> "And you're wasting your time with that foolish knight—"

SIR ANDREW

> (whispering) That's me, I bet.

MALVOLIO

> "That Sir Andrew—"

SIR ANDREW
(*aside*) I knew 'twas I, for many do call me fool.

MALVOLIO
(*seeing the letter*) What employment have we here?

FABIAN
(*aside*) Now is the woodcock near the gin.

SIR TOBY BELCH
75   (*aside*) O, peace! And the spirit of humors intimate reading aloud to him!

MALVOLIO
(picking up the letter) By my life, this is my lady's hand these be her very C's, her U's and her T's and thus makes she her great P's. It is, in contempt of question, her hand.

SIR ANDREW
80   (*aside*) Her C's, her U's and her T's. Why that?

MALVOLIO
(*reads*) "To the unknown beloved, this, and my good wishes"—Her very phrases! By your leave, wax. Soft! And the impressure her Lucrece, with which she uses to seal. 'Tis my lady. To whom should this be?

FABIAN
85   (*aside*) This wins him, liver and all.

MALVOLIO
(*reads*)
        "Jove knows I love,
        But who?
        Lips, do not move;
        No man must know."

SIR ANDREW

(whispering) I knew he was talking about me. A lot of people call me foolish.

MALVOLIO

(seeing the letter) What's this?

FABIAN

(whispering) He's taking the bait.

SIR TOBY BELCH

(whispering) Shhh! I hope he reads it out loud, to make it funnier!

MALVOLIO

(picking up the letter) My goodness, this is my lady's handwriting! These are her C's, her U's and her T's, and that's how she makes her big P's. It's definitely her handwriting, no doubt about it.

This is an obscene joke: Malvolio unwittingly spells out "cut," Elizabethan slang for vagina, which is what she uses to make her "pees."

SIR ANDREW

(whispering) Her C's, her U's, and her T's. Why focus on that?

MALVOLIO

(reads) To my dear beloved who doesn't know I love him, I send you this letter with all my heart"—That's exactly how she talks! Excuse me, sealing wax. *(he breaks the seal)* Wait! This is the stamp my lady seals her letters with—it has a picture of Lucrece on it. This letter is from Olivia. Who is this written to?

FABIAN

(whispering) This'll get him.

MALVOLIO

(he reads)

God knows I love someone.
But who?
I can't let my lips say his name;
No man must know."

90   "No man must know." What follows? The numbers
      altered. "No man must know." If this should be thee,
      Malvolio?

SIR TOBY BELCH
      (*aside*) Marry, hang thee, brock!

MALVOLIO
      (*reads*)
      "I may command where I adore,
95   But silence, like a Lucrece knife,
      With bloodless stroke my heart doth gore;
      M.O.A.I. doth sway my life."

FABIAN
      (*aside*) A fustian riddle!

SIR TOBY BELCH
      (*aside*) Excellent wench, say I.

MALVOLIO
100   "M.O.A.I. doth sway my life." Nay, but first, let me see, let
      me see, let me see.

FABIAN
      (*aside*) What dish o' poison has she dressed him!

SIR TOBY BELCH
      (*aside*) And with what wing the staniel checks at it!

MALVOLIO
      "I may command where I adore." Why, she may command
105   me. I serve her, she is my lady. Why, this is evident to any
      formal capacity. There is no obstruction in this. And the
      end—what should that alphabetical position portend? If I
      could make that resemble something in me—Softly!
      M.O.A.I.—

SIR TOBY BELCH
110   (*aside*) O, ay, make up that.—He is now at a cold scent.

FABIAN
      (aside) Sowter will cry upon 't for all this, though it be as
      rank as a fox.

"No man must know." What comes after that? Look, the meter changes in her poem. "No man must know." What if this someone were you, Malvolio?

SIR TOBY BELCH

(whispering) Go hang yourself, you stinking badger!

MALVOLIO

(reading)

"I may order the one I love.
But silence, like a knife, cuts open my heart
With strokes that draw no blood.
M.O.A.I. rules my life."

FABIAN

(whispering) What a pretentious riddle!

SIR TOBY BELCH

(whispering) That Maria has outdone herself!

MALVOLIO

"M.O.A.I. rules my life." Hmm, let me see, let me see, let me see.

FABIAN

(whispering) What a dish of poison she's mixed for him!

SIR TOBY BELCH

(whispering) And look how willingly he's taking the bait.

MALVOLIO

"I may command the one I love." Well, she commands me. I'm her servant. She's my boss. Why, anyone can see what this means. There's no ambiguity here. But the end, what do those letters mean? If only I could somehow relate them to me! Hmm. M.O.A.I.—

SIR TOBY BELCH

(whispering) Oh, bad dog.—He's losing the scent!

FABIAN

(whispering) He'll find it again, no matter how much it stinks.

MALVOLIO
"M"—Malvolio. "M"—why, that begins my name.

FABIAN
(aside) Did not I say he would work it out? The cur is
115   excellent at faults.

MALVOLIO
"M." But then there is no consonancy in the sequel that
suffers under probation "A" should follow but "O" does.

FABIAN
(aside) And "O" shall end, I hope.

SIR TOBY BELCH
(aside) Ay, or I'll cudgel him and make him cry "O!"

MALVOLIO
120   And then "I" comes behind.

FABIAN
(aside) Ay, an you had any eye behind you, you might see
more detraction at your heels than fortunes before you.

MALVOLIO
"M.O.A.I." This simulation is not as the former, and yet to
crush this a little, it would bow to me, for every one of these
125   letters are in my name. Soft, here follows prose.

(reads)
"If this fall into thy hand, revolve. In my stars I am above
thee, but be not afraid of greatness. Some are born great,
some achieve greatness, and some have greatness thrust
upon 'em. Thy Fates open their hands. Let thy blood
130   and spirit embrace them. And, to inure thyself to what
thou art like to be, cast thy humble slough and appear
fresh. Be opposite with a kinsman, surly with servants.

MALVOLIO

"M"—Malvolio. "M"—why, that's the first letter in my name.

FABIAN

(whispering) Didn't I tell you he'd figure it out? This dog's excellent at following false leads.

MALVOLIO

"M." But then the next letter isn't the same. "A" should be next, but instead "O" comes next.

FABIAN

(whispering) And an "O" like a noose will end this, I hope.

SIR TOBY BELCH

(whispering) Yeah, or I'll beat him up and make him yell "Oh!"

MALVOLIO

And then the "I" comes next.

FABIAN

(whispering) If you had an I in the back of your head, you'd see trouble behind you.

MALVOLIO

M.O.A.I. This code's not as easy to crack as the other one. But if I shake it up a little it'll work, because every one of those letters is in my name. But wait, there's some prose after her poem.

(he reads)

"If this letter falls into your hands, think carefully about what it says. By my birth I rank above you, but don't be afraid of my greatness. Some are born great, some achieve greatness, and some have greatness thrust upon them. Your fate awaits you. Accept it in body and spirit. To get used to the life you'll most likely be leading soon, get rid of your low-class trappings. Show some eagerness for the new upscale lifestyle that's

135

Let thy tongue tang arguments of state. Put thyself into the trick of singularity. She thus advises thee that sighs for thee. Remember who commended thy yellow stockings and wished to see thee ever cross-gartered. I say, remember. Go to, thou art made, if thou desir'st to be so; if not, let me see thee a steward still, the fellow of servants, and not worthy to touch Fortune's fingers.

140

Farewell. She that would alter services with thee,

The Fortunate Unhappy"

Daylight and champaign discovers not more. This is open. I will be proud, I will read politic authors, I will baffle Sir Toby, I will wash off gross acquaintance, I will be point-

145

devise the very man. I do not now fool myself, to let imagination jade me, for every reason excites to this, that my lady loves me. She did commend my yellow stockings of late, she did praise my leg being cross-gartered, and in this she manifests herself to my love, and with a kind of

150

injunction, drives me to these habits of her liking. I thank my stars I am happy. I will be strange, stout, in yellow stockings, and cross-gartered, even with the swiftness of putting on. Jove and my stars be praised! Here is yet a postscript.

(reads)

155

"Thou canst not choose but know who I am. If thou entertainest my love, let it appear in thy smiling. Thy smiles become thee well. Therefore in my presence still smile, dear my sweet, I prithee."

waiting for you. Argue with a relative like a nobleman, and be rude to servants. Talk about politics and affairs of state, and act free and independent. The woman who advises you to do this loves you. Remember the woman who complimented you on your yellow stockings, and said she always wanted to see you with crisscrossing laces going up your legs—remember her. Go ahead. A happy new life is there if you want it. If you don't want it, just keep acting like a lowly servant who's not brave enough to grab the happiness there before him. Goodbye. Signed, she who would be your servant,

The Fortunate Unhappy."

This is as clear as sunlight in an open field. I'll do it. I'll be vain and proud, I'll read up on politics, I'll insult Sir Toby, I'll get rid of my lower-class friends, and I'll be the perfect man for her. I know I'm not fooling myself, or letting myself get carried away by my imagination, because every clue points to the fact that Lady Olivia loves me. She did compliment me on my yellow stockings recently, and she said she liked how the crisscross laces looked on my legs. That's her way of saying she loves me. Oh, I thank my lucky stars, I'm so happy. For her I'll be strange and condescending, and I'll put on my yellow stockings and crisscross laces right away. Thank God and my horoscope! Here's a postscript!.

(reads)

"You must have figured out who I am. If you love me, let me know by smiling at me. You're so attractive when you smile. Please smile whenever you're near me, my dearest darling."

Jove, I thank thee! I will smile. I will do everything that
160   thou wilt have me.

Exit

FABIAN
          I will not give my part of this sport for a pension of
          thousands to be paid from the Sophy.

SIR TOBY BELCH
          I could marry this wench for this device.

SIR ANDREW
          So could I too.

SIR TOBY BELCH
165   And ask no other dowry with her but such another jest.

SIR ANDREW
          Nor I neither.

Enter MARIA

FABIAN
          Here comes my noble gull-catcher.

SIR TOBY BELCH
          Wilt thou set thy foot o' my neck?

SIR ANDREW
          Or o' mine either?

SIR TOBY BELCH
170   Shall I play my freedom at tray-trip, and become thy
          bondslave?

SIR ANDREW
          I' faith, or I either?

SIR TOBY BELCH
          Why, thou hast put him in such a dream that when the
          image of it leaves him he must run mad.

Dear God, thank you! I'll do everything she wants me to do.

MALVOLIO exits.

FABIAN

I wouldn't have missed this even for a pension of thousands of pounds, to be paid by the shah of Persia.

SIR TOBY BELCH

I could marry that Maria for thinking this up.

SIR ANDREW

So could I.

SIR TOBY BELCH

And I wouldn't ask for any dowry except for her to play another trick like this one.

SIR ANDREW

Neither would I.

MARIA enters.

FABIAN

Here she comes, the brilliant fool-catcher.

SIR TOBY BELCH

May I kiss your feet?

SIR ANDREW

And I too?

SIR TOBY BELCH

Shall I be your slave?

SIR ANDREW

Me too.

SIR TOBY BELCH

You've made him so delusional he'll go crazy when he learns the truth.

MARIA

175   Nay, but say true, does it work upon him?

SIR TOBY BELCH

Like aqua vitae with a midwife.

MARIA

If you will then see the fruits of the sport, mark his first
approach before my lady. He will come to her in yellow
stockings, and 'tis a color she abhors, and cross-gartered, a
180   fashion she detests. And he will smile upon her, which will
now be so unsuitable to her disposition, being addicted to
a melancholy as she is, that it cannot but turn him into a
notable contempt. If you will see it, follow me.

SIR TOBY BELCH

To the gates of Tartar, thou most excellent devil of wit!

SIR ANDREW

185   I'll make one too.

Exeunt

MARIA

Did it really work?

SIR TOBY BELCH

Like medicine for a sick man.

MARIA

If you want to really have some fun, watch him next time he's near Lady Olivia. He'll show up in yellow stockings—she hates yellow—and with laces criss-crossing up his legs—she hates that style of dress—and he'll smile, which will go completely against her mood, since she's addicted to sadness now. She'll definitely get upset with him. If you want to watch, follow me.

SIR TOBY BELCH

I'd follow you to the gates of Hell, you sneaky little devil!

SIR ANDREW

I'll come too.

They all exit.

ACT THREE

SCENE 1

Enter VIOLA, *and the* FOOL *playing with a tabor*

VIOLA

Save thee, friend, and thy music. Dost thou live by thy
tabour?

FOOL

No, sir, I live by the church.

VIOLA

Art thou a churchman?

FOOL

5　No such matter, sir. I do live by the church; for I do live at
my house, and my house doth stand by the church.

VIOLA

So thou mayst say the king lies by a beggar if a beggar dwell
near him, or the church stands by thy tabor, if thy tabor
stand by the church.

FOOL

10　You have said, sir. To see this age! A sentence is but a
cheveril glove to a good wit. How quickly the wrong side
may be turned outward!

VIOLA

Nay, that's certain. They that dally nicely with words may
quickly make them wanton.

FOOL

15　I would therefore my sister had no name, sir.

VIOLA

Why, man?

ACT THREE

SCENE 1

VIOLA *and the* FOOL, *playing a drum, enter.*

VIOLA

God bless you, my friend, and your music too. Do you make your living by playing that drum?

FOOL

No, sir, I live by the church.

VIOLA

Oh, you're a clergyman?

FOOL

No, I live by the church because I live in a house, and my house is by the church.

VIOLA

You could just as easily say that a king sleeps near a beggar if the beggar lives near him, or that the church is supported by your drum because it "stands by" your drum.

FOOL

You're right, sir. What a wonderful time to be alive! Sentences can be turned inside out so easily nowadays!

VIOLA

That's true. People who fool around with words too much can make words act like whores—changing all the time, and immoral too.

FOOL

That's why I wish my sister didn't have a name, sir.

VIOLA

Why, man?

FOOL

Why, sir, her name's a word, and to dally with that word
might make my sister wanton. But, indeed, words are very
rascals since bonds disgraced them.

VIOLA

20   Thy reason, man?

FOOL

Troth, sir, I can yield you none without words, and words
are grown so false, I am loath to prove reason with them.

VIOLA

I warrant thou art a merry fellow and carest for nothing.

FOOL

Not so, sir, I do care for something. But in my conscience,
25   sir, I do not care for you. If that be to care for nothing, sir,
I would it would make you invisible.

VIOLA

Art not thou the Lady Olivia's fool?

FOOL

No, indeed, sir; the Lady Olivia has no folly. She will keep
no fool, sir, till she be married, and fools are as like
30   husbands as pilchards are to herrings; the husband's the
bigger: I am indeed not her fool, but her corrupter of words.

VIOLA

I saw thee late at the Count Orsino's.

FOOL

Foolery, sir, does walk about the orb like the sun. It shines
everywhere. I would be sorry, sir, but the fool should be as
35   oft with your master as with my mistress: I think I saw your
wisdom there.

FOOL

Well, her name's a word, and if you fooled around with it you might make her into a whore. But, you know, words have been rascals ever since people started using written contracts rather than their word of honor.

VIOLA

Why do you say that?

FOOL

Honestly, sir, I'd need to use words to explain why, and since words are so unreliable and false, I'd rather avoid using them in a serious discussion.

VIOLA

I bet you're a happy fellow who doesn't care about anything.

FOOL

You're wrong, sir, I do care about something. But I'll admit I don't care for you. If that means I don't care about anything, you should disappear right now, since you're nothing.

VIOLA

Aren't you Lady Olivia's fool?

FOOL

No, sir. Lady Olivia doesn't want to have anything to do with foolishness. So she won't have a fool until she gets married. Fools are to husbands as anchovies are to sardines—husbands are the bigger ones. I'm not her fool. I just make words into whores for her.

VIOLA

I saw you at Count Orsino's recently.

FOOL

I'm everywhere. Foolishness is all over the world, just like sunshine. I'd be sorry if people thought your master was less familiar with foolishness than my mistress is. I think I saw you there, you wise man.

VIOLA

Nay, an thou pass upon me, I'll no more with thee. Hold, there's expenses for thee.

FOOL

Now Jove, in his next commodity of hair, send thee a beard!

VIOLA

40   By my troth, I'll tell thee, I am almost sick for one, (aside) though I would not have it grow on my chin. (to fool) Is thy lady within?

FOOL

Would not a pair of these have bred, sir?

VIOLA

Yes, being kept together and put to use.

FOOL

45   I would play Lord Pandarus of Phrygia, sir, to bring a Cressida to this Troilus.

VIOLA

(giving him money) I understand you, sir. 'Tis well begged.

FOOL

The matter, I hope, is not great, sir, begging but a beggar. Cressida was a beggar. My lady is within, sir. I will construe
50   to them whence you come. Who you are and what you would are out of my welkin, I might say "element," but the word is overworn.

VIOLA

Oh no, if you're joking around with me, I'm leaving. Wait, here's a coin for you.

FOOL

Next time God sends out a shipment of hair, I hope he gives you a beard!

VIOLA

Oh, I know. Seriously, I'm dying for one, *(to herself)* I mean, I'm dying for a man who has a beard; I don't want one to grow on my chin. *(to the* FOOL*)* Is Lady Olivia inside?

FOOL

If I had two of these coins, do you think they'd breed more coins?

VIOLA

Yes, if you kept them together and invested them.

FOOL

I'd like to be like that famous pimp, Lord Pandarus, and get a Cressida for my Troilus.

A "Cressida for my Troilus" means "a female coin for my male coin." Troilus and Cressida were famous lovers, brought together by Cressida's uncle Pandarus, traditionally regarded as the first pimp.

VIOLA

(giving the FOOL *money)* I get what you're driving at, sir. You're a very clever beggar.

FOOL

It shouldn't be too much to ask; I'm only begging for a beggar. They say Cressida became a beggar in her old age. My lady Olivia's inside, sir. I'll tell them where you come from, though I don't know who you are or what you want. I'd say I was "out of my element," but that phrase is overused, so I'll say I'm "out of my air."

Exit

VIOLA
> This fellow is wise enough to play the fool,
> And to do that well craves a kind of wit.
55 > He must observe their mood on whom he jests,
> The quality of persons, and the time,
> And, like the haggard, check at every feather
> That comes before his eye. This is a practise
> As full of labor as a wise man's art,
60 > For folly that he wisely shows is fit.
> But wise men, folly-fall'n, quite taint their wit.

Enter SIR TOBY BELCH, *and* SIR ANDREW

SIR TOBY BELCH
> Save you, gentleman.

VIOLA
> And you, sir.

SIR ANDREW
> *Dieu vous garde, monsieur.*

VIOLA
65 > *Et vous aussi. Votre serviteur!*

SIR ANDREW
> I hope, sir, you are, and I am yours.

SIR TOBY BELCH
> Will you encounter the house? My niece is desirous you
> should enter, if your trade be to her.

VIOLA
> I am bound to your niece, sir. I mean, she is the list of my
70 > voyage.

SIR TOBY BELCH
> Taste your legs, sir. Put them to motion.

The FOOL exits.

VIOLA

This guy's wise enough to play the fool, and only clever people can do that. He pays attention to the mood and social rank of the person he's joking with, and also to the time of day. And he doesn't let go of his target when a distraction appears. His job requires as much effort and skill as any wise man's occupation could. And he shows he's very smart at playing the fool, while smart people look stupid when they play the fool.

SIR TOBY BELCH *and* SIR ANDREW *enter.*

SIR TOBY BELCH

Hello, sir.

VIOLA

Hello to you too, sir.

SIR ANDREW

(speaking in French) May God protect you, sir.

VIOLA

(speaking in French) And you too, sir. I'm at your service.

SIR ANDREW

(stammering) Oh, good, I am too.

Sir Andrew's awkwardness reveals that he's bad at French.

SIR TOBY BELCH

My niece would like you to come in to the house, if your business here has to do with her.

VIOLA

I'm headed for your niece, sir. She's the reason I'm here.

SIR TOBY BELCH

Taste your legs, sir. Please go inside.

VIOLA

My legs do better understand me, sir, than I understand
what you mean by bidding me taste my legs.

SIR TOBY BELCH

I mean, to go, sir, to enter.

VIOLA

75   I will answer you with gait and entrance. But we are
prevented.

Enter OLIVIA *and* MARIA

Most excellent accomplished lady, the heavens rain odors
on you!

SIR ANDREW

(*aside*) That youth's a rare courtier. "Rain odors." Well.

VIOLA

80   My matter hath no voice, lady, but to your own most
pregnant and vouchsafed ear.

SIR ANDREW

(*aside*) "Odors," "pregnant," and "vouchsafed." I'll get
'em all three all ready.

OLIVIA

Let the garden door be shut, and leave me to my hearing.

Exeunt SIR TOBY BELCH, SIR ANDREW, *and* MARIA

85   Give me your hand, sir.

VIOLA

My duty, madam, and most humble service.

OLIVIA

What is your name?

VIOLA

> Taste my legs? My legs stand under me, but I don't understand what "taste your legs" means.

SIR TOBY BELCH

> I mean please go into the house, sir.

VIOLA

> I will. But now we don't have to!

OLIVIA *and* MARIA *enter.*

> Oh, beautiful and accomplished lady, may the heavens rain odors upon you!

SIR ANDREW

> *(to himself)* That young man's classy. "Rain odors." That's good.

VIOLA

> My message is not for anyone else to hear, my lady. It's only for your willing and receptive ear.

SIR ANDREW

> *(to himself)* "Odors," "willing," and "deserving." I'll have to remember those words so I can use them later myself.

OLIVIA

> Close the garden door and leave me alone to hear his message.

SIR TOBY BELCH, SIR ANDREW, *and* MARIA *exit.*

> Give me your hand, sir.

VIOLA

> I give you my obedience and my humble service, madam.

OLIVIA

> What's your name?

VIOLA

>Cesario is your servant's name, fair princess.

OLIVIA

>My servant, sir! 'Twas never merry world
>
90 >Since lowly feigning was call'd compliment.
>You're servant to the Count Orsino, youth.

VIOLA

>And he is yours, and his must needs be yours:
>Your servant's servant is your servant, madam.

OLIVIA

>For him, I think not on him. For his thoughts,
>
95 >Would they were blanks, rather than fill'd with me.

VIOLA

>Madam, I come to whet your gentle thoughts
>On his behalf.

OLIVIA

>   O, by your leave, I pray you,
>I bade you never speak again of him.
>But, would you undertake another suit,
>
100 >I had rather hear you to solicit that
>Than music from the spheres.

VIOLA

>   Dear lady—

OLIVIA

>Give me leave, beseech you. I did send,
>After the last enchantment you did here,
>A ring in chase of you. So did I abuse
>
105 >Myself, my servant, and, I fear me, you:
>Under your hard construction must I sit,
>To force that on you, in a shameful cunning
>Which you knew none of yours. What might you think?

VIOLA

Cesario is my name—your servant's name—fair princess.

OLIVIA

My servant! The world's gone downhill since fake humility started passing for compliments. You're not my servant, young man. You're Count Orsino's servant.

VIOLA

But he's your servant, so everything that's his must be yours too. Your servant's servant is your servant, madam.

OLIVIA

As for him, I never think about him. As for his thoughts, I wish he'd think about nothing at all rather than think about me all the time.

VIOLA

Madam, I've come here to try to make you like him.

OLIVIA

Oh, please, I'm begging you, don't mention him again. But if you want to tell me that someone else loves me, I'd enjoy hearing that more than I'd enjoy listening to angels sing.

VIOLA

My dear lady—

OLIVIA

Please let me say something, I'm begging you. After you cast your magic spell on me last time, I sent you a ring. I fear it was a mistake, since I tricked my servant, myself, and you too. You probably think poorly of me after I forced that ring on you with such outrageous trickery. What else could you possibly think of me?

Have you not set mine honor at the stake,
110 And baited it with all the unmuzzled thoughts
That tyrannous heart can think? To one of your receiving
Enough is shown. A cypress, not a bosom,
Hides my heart. So, let me hear you speak.

VIOLA
I pity you.

OLIVIA
That's a degree to love.

VIOLA
115 No, not a grize. For 'tis a vulgar proof
That very oft we pity enemies.

OLIVIA
Why then methinks 'tis time to smile again.
O world, how apt the poor are to be proud!
If one should be a prey, how much the better
120 To fall before the lion than the wolf! (*clock strikes*)
The clock upbraids me with the waste of time.
Be not afraid, good youth, I will not have you.
And yet when wit and youth is come to harvest,
Your wife is like to reap a proper man.
125 There lies your way, due west.

VIOLA
Then westward ho!
Grace and good disposition attend your ladyship!
You'll nothing, madam, to my lord by me?

OLIVIA
Stay, I prithee, tell me what thou thinkest of me.

VIOLA
That you do think you are not what you are.

OLIVIA
130 If I think so, I think the same of you.

VIOLA
Then think you right: I am not what I am.

OLIVIA
I would you were as I would have you be!

Haven't you totally dismissed my honor and integrity in your anger? For someone as intelligent as you the situation must be clear enough. I'm wearing my heart on my sleeve, and I can't hide my feelings. So let me hear what you have to say.

VIOLA

I feel sorry for you.

OLIVIA

That's a step in the direction of love.

VIOLA

No, not at all. It's a perfectly ordinary experience for us to feel sorry for our enemies.

OLIVIA

Well, enough of my whining then. That's that! I was getting carried away with fantasies I didn't deserve to have. But I should consider myself lucky. It's much better to be destroyed by a noble enemy than by a cruel and heartless one. *(a clock strikes)* Listen to that, the clock's scolding me for wasting my time loving you. Don't worry, young man, I won't stalk you. And when you're older and wiser and ready for marriage, your future wife will have a fine husband. There's the way back home for you, due west.

VIOLA

Then west is where I'm headed! I wish you all the best. You do

OLIVIA

Stay, Please, tell me what you think of me.

VIOLA

I think you're denying what you really are.

OLIVIA

If that's true, I think the same thing about you.

VIOLA

You're right. I am not what I am.

OLIVIA

I wish you were what I wanted you to be!

VIOLA

> Would it be better, madam, than I am?
> I wish it might, for now I am your fool.

OLIVIA

135 > *(aside)* Oh, what a deal of scorn looks beautiful
> In the contempt and anger of his lip!
> A murderous guilt shows not itself more soon
> Than love that would seem hid. Love's night is noon.
> *(to* **VIOLA***)* Cesario, by the roses of the spring,
140 > By maidhood, honor, truth, and everything,
> I love thee so, that, maugre all thy pride,
> Nor wit nor reason can my passion hide.
> Do not extort thy reasons from this clause,
> For that I woo, thou therefore hast no cause,
145 > But rather reason thus with reason fetter.
> Love sought is good, but given unsought better.

VIOLA

> By innocence I swear, and by my youth
> I have one heart, one bosom, and one truth,
> And that no woman has, nor never none
150 > Shall mistress be of it, save I alone.
> And so adieu, good madam. Nevermore
> Will I my master's tears to you deplore.

OLIVIA

> Yet come again, for thou perhaps mayst move
> That heart, which now abhors, to like his love.

Exeunt

VIOLA

Would it be better if I were that, instead of what I am? I wish I were something better, because right now I'm a big fool.

OLIVIA

(to herself) Oh, how beautiful he is even when he's angry and full of contempt! A murderer can hide his guilt longer than someone in love can hide her love. Love shines brightly and can't be hidden. *(to* **VIOLA***)* Cesario, I swear by the spring roses, by virginity, honor, truth, and everything, I swear I love you. I love you so much that I can't hide my passion for you, as clever as I am. Don't assume that because I'm pursuing you there's no reason to pursue me. Put two and two together and realize that asking for love is good, but getting it without asking is much better.

VIOLA

And I swear by my youth and innocence that I've only got one heart and one love to give, and that I've never given them to a woman and never will. So goodbye, my lady. I won't ever come to complain about my lord's love for you again.

OLIVIA

Then come again for another reason. You might still be able to make yourself fall in love with me, the person he loves, even though you hate me now.

They exit.

ACT 3, SCENE 2

Enter SIR TOBY BELCH, SIR ANDREW, *and* FABIAN

SIR ANDREW
No, faith, I'll not stay a jot longer.

SIR TOBY BELCH
Thy reason, dear venom, give thy reason.

FABIAN
5   You must needs yield your reason, Sir Andrew.

SIR ANDREW
Marry, I saw your niece do more favors to the Count's
servingman than ever she bestowed upon me. I saw 't i' the
orchard.

SIR TOBY BELCH
Did she see thee the while, old boy? Tell me that.

SIR ANDREW
10   As plain as I see you now.

FABIAN
This was a great argument of love in her toward you.

SIR ANDREW
'Slight, will you make an ass o' me?

FABIAN
I will prove it legitimate, sir, upon the oaths of judgment
and reason.

SIR TOBY BELCH
15   And they have been grand-jurymen since before Noah was
a sailor.

FABIAN
She did show favor to the youth in your sight only to
exasperate you, to awake your dormouse valor, to put fire in
your heart and brimstone in your liver. You should then
20   have accosted her, and with some excellent jests, fire-new
from the mint, you should have banged the youth into
dumbness.

ACT 3, SCENE 2

SIR TOBY BELCH, SIR ANDREW, *and* FABIAN *enter.*

SIR ANDREW
No, I won't stay a second longer.

SIR TOBY BELCH
Why are you leaving, my angry friend?

FABIAN
Yes, you have to tell us why, Sir Andrew.

SIR ANDREW
Well, because I saw your niece Olivia treat the count's messenger better than she's ever treated me. I saw it in the orchard.

SIR TOBY BELCH
Did she see you there the whole time, old boy? Tell me that.

SIR ANDREW
Yes, she saw me quite clearly.

FABIAN
Well, that proves she's in love with you.

SIR ANDREW
Are you trying to make fun of me?

FABIAN
No, I'll prove it with airtight evidence and logical argument.

SIR TOBY BELCH
And you can't deny evidence and argument— They've been around since Noah's ark.

FABIAN
She flirted with the messenger boy to exasperate you, fire up your passions, and make you angry and jealous. You should have run up to her, unleashed a few excellent quips invented on the spot, and rendered the young man speechless.

This was looked for at your hand, and this was balked. The
double gilt of this opportunity you let time wash off, and
25   you are now sailed into the north of my lady's opinion,
where you will hang like an icicle on a Dutchman's beard,
unless you do redeem it by some laudable attempt either of
valor or policy.

SIR ANDREW

An 't be any way, it must be with valor, for policy I hate. I
30   had as lief be a Brownist as a politician.

SIR TOBY BELCH

Why, then, build me thy fortunes upon the basis of valor.
Challenge me the count's youth to fight with him. Hurt him
in eleven places. My niece shall take note of it, and assure
thyself, there is no love-broker in the world can more
35   prevail in man's commendation with woman than report of
valor.

FABIAN

There is no way but this, Sir Andrew.

SIR ANDREW

Will either of you bear me a challenge to him?

SIR TOBY BELCH

Go, write it in a martial hand. Be curst and brief. It is no
40   matter how witty, so it be eloquent and full of invention.
Taunt him with the license of ink. If thou "thou"-est him
some thrice, it shall not be amiss; and as many lies as will lie
in thy sheet of paper, although the sheet were big enough
for the bed of Ware in England, set 'em down. Go, about it.
45   Let there be gall enough in thy ink, though thou write with
a goose-pen, no matter. About it.

SIR ANDREW

Where shall I find you?

That's what she was expecting, and you let her down. You wasted a golden opportunity, and now my lady thinks badly of you. You can only raise her opinion of you with some impressive act of courage or complicated intrigue.

SIR ANDREW

I'll have to do something courageous then, because I hate intrigue. I'd rather be a heretic than a schemer with fancy plots.

SIR TOBY BELCH

Well then, improve your situation with a show of courage. Challenge the count's young servant to a fight. Hurt him in eleven different places. My niece Olivia will notice, and let me tell you, no matchmaker in the world can get you a woman faster than a reputation for courage.

FABIAN

It's really the only way, Sir Andrew.

SIR ANDREW

Will either of you give him the message that I'm challenging him to a duel?

SIR TOBY BELCH

Go ahead and write it down. Make your handwriting look like a soldier's. Be pointed and brief. It doesn't need to be witty as long as it's eloquent and imaginative. Taunt him as much as you want, since you're only doing it in writing. It's fine if you refer to him as "thou" instead of "you." Write down as many lies as you can fit on a sheet of paper. Go ahead, get on with it. You may be using an ordinary pen, but you can fill it with poison ink. Now get busy.

"Thou" was an informal version of "you," and thus insulting when used to an aristocrat.

SIR ANDREW

Where will I find you when I've finished it?

SIR TOBY BELCH
> We'll call thee at the cubiculo. Go.

Exit SIR ANDREW

FABIAN
> This is a dear manikin to you, Sir Toby.

SIR TOBY BELCH
50 > I have been dear to him, lad, some two thousand strong,
> or so.

FABIAN
> We shall have a rare letter from him: but you'll not
> deliver 't?

SIR TOBY BELCH
> Never trust me, then. And by all means stir on the youth to
55 > an answer. I think oxen and wainropes cannot hale them
> together. For Andrew, if he were opened and you find so
> much blood in his liver as will clog the foot of a flea, I'll eat
> the rest of the anatomy.

FABIAN
> And his opposite, the youth, bears in his visage no great
60 > presage of cruelty.

Enter MARIA

SIR TOBY BELCH
> Look where the youngest wren of nine comes.

MARIA
> If you desire the spleen, and will laugh yourself into
> stitches, follow me. Yond gull Malvolio is turned heathen,
> a very renegado. For there is no Christian that means to be
65 > saved by believing rightly can ever believe such impossible
> passages of grossness. He's in yellow stockings.

SIR TOBY BELCH

We'll come find you in the bedroom. Go on.

SIR ANDREW exits.

FABIAN

This precious little guy is putty in your hands, Sir Toby.

SIR TOBY BELCH

He must like me, since he's let me spend two thousand of his ducats.

FABIAN

His letter's going to be hilarious. But you're not going to deliver it, are you?

SIR TOBY BELCH

Never trust me again if I don't. And by all means see *It was commonly* if you can get the young man to answer it. I don't think *believed that* a team of oxen could get them close enough to fight. If *cowards had white* you dissected Andrew and found enough red blood in *livers with no* his liver for a flea to eat, then I'd eat the rest of his *blood in them.* corpse. He's a coward.

FABIAN

And his opponent, the young messenger, doesn't look like he'd be very aggressive in a fight.

MARIA enters.

SIR TOBY BELCH

Here comes my little bird.

MARIA

Listen, if you want a good laugh—and I mean a side-splitting one—then follow me. That gullible idiot Malvolio must have renounced Christianity, since no Christian could do such outrageous things as he's doing. He's wearing yellow stockings.

SIR TOBY BELCH
> And cross-gartered?

MARIA
> Most villanously, like a pedant that keeps a school i' the
> church. I have dogged him, like his murderer. He does obey
70   every point of the letter that I dropped to betray him. He
> does smile his face into more lines than is in the new map
> with the augmentation of the Indies. You have not seen such
> a thing as 'tis. I can hardly forbear hurling things at him. I
> know my lady will strike him. If she do, he'll smile and take
75   't for a great favor.

SIR TOBY BELCH
> Come, bring us, bring us where he is.

Exeunt

SIR TOBY BELCH

> With crisscrossed laces?

MARIA

> Oh, he looks like a pathetic Sunday school teacher.
> I've stalked him like a murderer, and he's done every-
> thing the letter told him to. He smiles so much his face
> has more lines in it than a map of the East Indies.
> You've never seen anything like it. I can hardly keep
> myself from throwing things at him. I know that my
> lady's going to end up hitting him. And when she
> does, he'll imagine she's flirting with him.

SIR TOBY BELCH

> Come on, take us to him.

> *They all exit.*

ACT 3, SCENE 3

Enter SEBASTIAN *and* ANTONIO

SEBASTIAN
I would not by my will have troubled you,
But, since you make your pleasure of your pains,
I will no further chide you.

ANTONIO
5 I could not stay behind you. My desire,
More sharp than filèd steel, did spur me forth.
And not all love to see you, though so much
As might have drawn one to a longer voyage,
But jealousy what might befall your travel,
10 Being skilless in these parts, which to a stranger,
Unguided and unfriended, often prove
Rough and unhospitable. My willing love,
The rather by these arguments of fear,
Set forth in your pursuit.

SEBASTIAN
                                My kind Antonio,
15 I can no other answer make but thanks,
And thanks, and ever thanks. And oft good turns
Are shuffled off with such uncurrent pay.
But were my worth as is my conscience, firm,
You should find better dealing. What's to do?
20 Shall we go see the relics of this town?

ANTONIO
Tomorrow, sir. Best first go see your lodging.

SEBASTIAN
I am not weary, and 'tis long to night:
I pray you, let us satisfy our eyes
With the memorials and the things of fame
25 That do renown this city.

ACT 3, SCENE 3

SEBASTIAN *and* ANTONIO *enter.*

SEBASTIAN

I really didn't want to inconvenience you. But since you seem to enjoy helping me, I won't nag you to stop any more.

ANTONIO

I couldn't stay behind after you left. I just felt a sharp desire to follow you. It wasn't just that I wanted to see you, though I very much did want that. I was also worried about what might happen to you while you were traveling, since you're not familiar with this area, and it's rough and unwelcoming to a stranger with no guide. I followed you because I love you and I was worried about you.

SEBASTIAN

My friend Antonio, all I can say is thank you. I know words are cheap. If I had any money I'd back up my gratitude with cash. Anyway, what should we do? Should we go see the sights in the town?

ANTONIO

We can do that tomorrow, sir. First we should make sure you have somewhere to stay.

SEBASTIAN

I'm not tired, and night is a long time away. Come on, let's go see the sights.

ANTONIO

Would you'd pardon me;

I do not without danger walk these streets:
Once in a sea-fight 'gainst the Count his galleys
I did some service, of such note indeed,
That were I ta'en here it would scarce be answered.

SEBASTIAN

30   Belike you slew great number of his people?

ANTONIO

The offence is not of such a bloody nature;
Albeit the quality of the time and quarrel
Might well have given us bloody argument.
It might have since been answered in repaying
35   What we took from them, which, for traffic's sake,
Most of our city did. Only myself stood out;
For which, if I be lapsèd in this place,
I shall pay dear.

SEBASTIAN

Do not then walk too open.

ANTONIO

It doth not fit me. Hold, sir, here's my purse.
(giving him money)
40   In the south suburbs, at the Elephant,
Is best to lodge. I will bespeak our diet,
Whiles you beguile the time and feed your knowledge
With viewing of the town. There shall you have me.

SEBASTIAN

Why I your purse?

ANTONIO

45   Haply your eye shall light upon some toy
You have desire to purchase, and your store,
I think, is not for idle markets, sir.

SEBASTIAN

I'll be your purse-bearer and leave you
For an hour.

ANTONIO

I'm sorry, but I can't. You see, it's dangerous for me to walk in these streets. Once in a battle at sea I did a lot of damage to Count Orsino's warships. If they arrested me here, it'd be the end of me.

SEBASTIAN

You probably killed a lot of his men?

ANTONIO

No, I didn't do anything as violent as that, though we would've been justified in shedding a little blood over the matter. The whole quarrel might have been resolved since then when we repaid what we stole from them—which most of our city did, for the sake of friendly trade relations. I was the only one who refused to give back what I stole. That's why I'll pay dearly if they find me here.

SEBASTIAN

Then don't make yourself too conspicuous.

ANTONIO

You're right. Hang on a minute, here's some money for you. *(he gives SEBASTIAN money)* The best place to stay around here is an inn called the Elephant, in the suburbs south of the city. I'll arrange for our meals while you enjoy yourself and educate yourself by looking at the town. You'll find me at the Elephant.

SEBASTIAN

Why are you giving me your purse?

ANTONIO

Maybe you'll see some little trinket you want to buy. I doubt you've got enough money for little purchases like that.

SEBASTIAN

I'll hold on to your money and leave you for an hour.

ANTONIO
                    To the Elephant.

SEBASTIAN
                                        I do remember.

                                                        Exeunt

ANTONIO

We'll meet at the Elephant.

SEBASTIAN

I remember.

They exit.

ACT 3, SCENE 4

Enter OLIVIA *and* MARIA

OLIVIA
I have sent after him. He says he'll come.
How shall I feast him? What bestow of him?
For youth is bought more oft than begged or borrow'd.
I speak too loud.—
5   Where's Malvolio? He is sad and civil
And suits well for a servant with my fortunes.
Where is Malvolio?

MARIA
He's coming, madam; but in very strange manner. He is
sure possessed, madam.

OLIVIA
10   Why, what's the matter? Does he rave?

MARIA
No, madam, he does nothing but smile. Your ladyship were
best to have some guard about you if he come, for sure the
man is tainted in 's wits.

OLIVIA
Go call him hither.

Exit MARIA

I am as mad as he,
15   If sad and merry madness equal be.

Enter MARIA, *with* MALVOLIO

How now, Malvolio?

MALVOLIO
Sweet lady, ho, ho.

ACT 3, SCENE 4

OLIVIA *and* MARIA *enter.*

OLIVIA

I've sent for him. He says he'll come. What kind of food should I serve him? What presents should I give him? It's easier to buy young people than to beg or borrow them. Oh, I'm talking too loud.—Where's Malvolio? He's very serious, which is right for someone in mourning like me. Where is Malvolio?

MARIA

He's coming, madam; but he's acting very strangely. He must be possessed by the devil.

OLIVIA

Why, what's the matter with him? Is he talking nonsense?

MARIA

No, he just smiles. You should have a guard nearby if he comes in here, because he's clearly disturbed.

OLIVIA

Ask him in here.

MARIA *exits.*

I'm as crazy as he is, if sad craziness and happy craziness are equivalent.

MARIA *enters with* MALVOLIO.

What's going on, Malvolio?

MALVOLIO

Hello, sweet lady.

OLIVIA
Smilest thou? I sent for thee upon a sad occasion.

MALVOLIO
Sad, lady! I could be sad. This does make some obstruction
20   in the blood, this cross-gartering, but what of that? If it
please the eye of one, it is with me as the very true sonnet is,
"Please one, and please all."

OLIVIA
Why, how dost thou, man? What is the matter with thee?

MALVOLIO
Not black in my mind, though yellow in my legs. It did
25   come to his hands, and commands shall be executed. I
think we do know the sweet Roman hand.

OLIVIA
Wilt thou go to bed, Malvolio?

MALVOLIO
To bed? "Ay, sweetheart, and I'll come to thee."

OLIVIA
God comfort thee! Why dost thou smile so, and kiss thy
30   hand so oft?

MARIA
How do you, Malvolio?

MALVOLIO
At your request! Yes, nightingales answer daws!

MARIA
Why appear you with this ridiculous boldness before my
lady?

MALVOLIO
35   "Be not afraid of greatness." 'Twas well writ.

OLIVIA
What meanest thou by that, Malvolio?

MALVOLIO
"Some are born great—"

OLIVIA

You're smiling? I sent for you about a sad occasion.

MALVOLIO

Sad, my lady! I could be sad if I wanted to be. These crisscrossing laces do cut off the circulation in my legs a bit, but who cares? As the sonnet says, "If you please one special person, you please everyone who matters."

OLIVIA

Why, what's going on? What's the matter with you?

MALVOLIO

My legs may be yellow, but I don't feel blue. It was addressed to him, and orders must be obeyed. I think we know whose fancy handwriting that was.

OLIVIA

Don't you think you should go to bed, Malvolio?

MALVOLIO

To bed! "Yes, sweetheart, I'll come to you."

OLIVIA

For heaven's sake, why are you smiling like that and kissing your hand so much?

MARIA

How are you feeling, Malvolio?

MALVOLIO

You're asking me! Noble people don't answer to peasants!

MARIA

Why are you acting so brazen toward my lady?

MALVOLIO

"Don't be afraid of greatness." That was well written.

OLIVIA

What do you mean by that, Malvolio?

MALVOLIO

"Some are born great—"

OLIVIA
Ha?

MALVOLIO
"Some achieve greatness—"

OLIVIA
40   What sayest thou?

MALVOLIO
"And some have greatness thrust upon them."

OLIVIA
Heaven restore thee!

MALVOLIO
"Remember who commended thy yellow stockings—"

OLIVIA
Thy yellow stockings?

MALVOLIO
45   "And wished to see thee cross-gartered."

OLIVIA
Cross-gartered?

MALVOLIO
"Go to, thou art made, if thou desirest to be so—"

OLIVIA
Am I made?

MALVOLIO
"If not, let me see thee a servant still."

OLIVIA
50   Why, this is very midsummer madness.

Enter SERVANT

SERVANT
Madam, the young gentleman of the Count Orsino's is
returned. I could hardly entreat him back. He attends your
ladyship's pleasure.

OLIVIA

What?

MALVOLIO

"Some achieve greatness—"

OLIVIA

What are you saying?

MALVOLIO

"And some have greatness thrust upon them."

OLIVIA

Heaven help you!

MALVOLIO

"Remember who liked your yellow stockings—"

OLIVIA

Your yellow stockings?

MALVOLIO

"And wanted to see you with laces crisscrossed over your legs."

OLIVIA

Crisscrossed?

MALVOLIO

"Go ahead. A happy new life is there if you want it—"

OLIVIA

Am I a new life?

MALVOLIO

"If you don't want it, just keep acting like a lowly servant."

OLIVIA

This is completely insane.

SERVANT *enters.*

SERVANT

Madam, Count Orsino's young messenger has returned. It was hard to get him to come back, but he's here now, waiting for you.

OLIVIA
I'll come to him.

Exit SERVANT

55   Good Maria, let this fellow be looked to. Where's my
        cousin Toby? Let some of my people have a special care of
        him. I would not have him miscarry for the half of my
        dowry.

Exeunt OLIVIA *and* MARIA

MALVOLIO
Oh, ho! Do you come near me now? No worse man than Sir
60   Toby to look to me. This concurs directly with the letter.
        She sends him on purpose that I may appear stubborn to
        him, for she incites me to that in the letter. "Cast thy
        humble slough," says she. "Be opposite with a kinsman,
        surly with servants. Let thy tongue tang with arguments of
65   state. Put thyself into the trick of singularity," and
        consequently sets down the manner how: as, a sad face, a
        reverend carriage, a slow tongue, in the habit of some sir of
        note, and so forth. I have limed her, but it is Jove's doing,
        and Jove make me thankful! And when she went away now,
70   "Let this fellow be looked to." "Fellow!" Not "Malvolio,"
        nor after my degree, but "fellow." Why, everything adheres
        together, that no dram of a scruple, no scruple of a scruple,
        no obstacle, no incredulous or unsafe circumstance—what
        can be said? Nothing that can be can come between me and
75   the full prospect of my hopes. Well, Jove, not I, is the doer
        of this, and he is to be thanked.

Enter MARIA, *with* SIR TOBY BELCH *and* FABIAN

OLIVIA

I'll go to him.

SERVANT *exits.*

Maria, take care of this poor fellow here. Where's my cousin Toby? Have some of my servants take care of Malvolio. I'd give half my dowry to keep anything bad from happening to him.

OLIVIA *and* MARIA *exit.*

MALVOLIO

Oh ho! Look at me now! No less a person than Sir Toby, Lady Olivia's own relative, is going to take care of me. This is just what the letter said. She's sending him to me on purpose, so I can be rude to him just like she said in the letter. "Get rid of your low-class trapping," she said. "Argue with a relative of mine like a nobleman, and be rude to servants. Talk about politics and affairs of state, and act free and independent." And then she explains how to do it: I should have a serious face and dignified demeanor, well-modulated speech, acting like a distinguished gentleman and so on. I've got her now, but I've got God to thank for it! And when she left just now, she said "Take care of this poor fellow here." Fellow!" Not "Malvolio," not anything referring to my low station in life, but "fellow." Everything's going perfectly. Not the tiniest ounce, not the littlest insignificant amount of trouble or bad luck could ruin it—what can I say? Nothing can come between me and the fulfillment of all my hopes. Well, God is responsible for that, not me, and he deserves thanks.

MARIA *enters with* SIR TOBY BELCH *and* FABIAN.

SIR TOBY BELCH

Which way is he, in the name of sanctity? If all the devils of
hell be drawn in little, and Legion himself possessed him,
yet I'll speak to him.

FABIAN

80   Here he is, here he is. How is 't with you, sir? How is't with
you, man?

MALVOLIO

Go off, I discard you. Let me enjoy my private. Go off.

MARIA

(to SIR TOBY BELCH) Lo, how hollow the fiend speaks within
him! Did not I tell you? Sir Toby, my lady prays you to have
85   a care of him.

MALVOLIO

Aha! Does she so?

SIR TOBY BELCH

(to FABIAN and MARIA) Go to, go to! Peace, peace. We must
deal gently with him. Let me alone.—How do you,
Malvolio? How is 't with you? What, man, defy the devil!
90   Consider, he's an enemy to mankind.

MALVOLIO

Do you know what you say?

MARIA

(to SIR TOBY BELCH) La you, an you speak ill of the devil,
how he takes it at heart! Pray God, he be not bewitched!

FABIAN

Carry his water to the wisewoman.

MARIA

95   Marry, and it shall be done tomorrow morning if I live. My
lady would not lose him for more than I'll say.

MALVOLIO

How now, mistress?

SIR TOBY BELCH

Where is he, for God's sake? I don't care if all the devils in hell crammed together to possess him, I still want to speak to him.

FABIAN

Here he is, here he is. How are you, sir?

MALVOLIO

Go away. I don't want to see your face. Let me enjoy my privacy. Go away.

MARIA

(to SIR TOBY BELCH) Ooh, listen to the scary devil speaking from inside him! Didn't I tell you? Sir Toby, Lady Olivia wants you to take care of him.

MALVOLIO

Ah-ha! Does she?

SIR TOBY BELCH

(to FABIAN and MARIA) Come on, come on! Calm down, calm down. We need to treat him gently. Let me take care of this.—How are you, Malvolio? How are things? Come on, man, just say no to the devil! Think about it, he's the enemy of mankind.

MALVOLIO

Do you even know what you're talking about?

MARIA

(to SIR TOBY BELCH) Look at that, he acts insulted if you say bad things about the devil! I hope to God he's not bewitched!

FABIAN

Get a urine sample and take it to a witch doctor to find out.

MARIA

Sure thing, we'll do it tomorrow morning. My lady would never want to lose him.

MALVOLIO

What are you saying, mistress?

MARIA
> O Lord!

SIR TOBY BELCH
> *(to* MARIA*)* Prithee, hold thy peace. This is not the way. Do
> you not see you move him? Let me alone with him.

FABIAN
> No way but gentleness, gently, gently. The fiend is rough
> and will not be roughly used.

SIR TOBY BELCH
> *(to* MALVOLIO*)* Why, how now, my bawcock! How dost thou,
> chuck?

MALVOLIO
> Sir!

SIR TOBY BELCH
> Ay, Biddy, come with me.—What, man! 'Tis not for
> gravity to play at cherry-pit with Satan. Hang him, foul
> collier!

MARIA
> Get him to say his prayers, good Sir Toby, get him to pray.

MALVOLIO
> My prayers, minx?

MARIA
> *(to* SIR TOBY BELCH*)* No, I warrant you, he will not hear of
> godliness.

MALVOLIO
> Go, hang yourselves all! You are idle, shallow things. I am
> not of your element. You shall know more hereafter.

Exit

MARIA

Oh, Lord!

SIR TOBY BELCH

(to MARIA) Please, keep quiet. This is not the way to act. Don't you see you're upsetting him? Leave me alone with him.

FABIAN

Gentleness is the only way to go—gently, gently. The devil inside him is rough, but we can't treat it roughly.

SIR TOBY BELCH

(to the imaginary devil inside MALVOLIO) So how are you, my pretty little bird? How are you doing in there, sweet little chicken?

MALVOLIO

Sir!

SIR TOBY BELCH

Yes, dear little chick, come along with me.—Shut up, man! You're serious enough to know not to play games with Satan. Damn that dirty black coalminer of a devil!

MARIA

Get him to say his prayers, Sir Toby, get him to pray.

MALVOLIO

My prayers, you hussy?

MARIA

(to SIR TOBY BELCH) No, I'm telling you, he refuses to hear anything about religion.

MALVOLIO

Go hang yourselves, all of you! You're all lazy and shallow. I'm not like you. I have a higher future waiting for me. You'll know more about it later.

MALVOLIO *exits.*

SIR TOBY BELCH
115   Is 't possible?

FABIAN
        If this were played upon a stage now, I could condemn it as
        an improbable fiction.

SIR TOBY BELCH
        His very genius hath taken the infection of the device, man.

MARIA
        Nay, pursue him now, lest the device take air and taint.

FABIAN
120   Why, we shall make him mad indeed.

MARIA
        The house will be the quieter.

SIR TOBY BELCH
        Come, we'll have him in a dark room and bound. My niece
        is already in the belief that he's mad. We may carry it thus,
        for our pleasure and his penance, till our very pastime, tired
125   out of breath, prompt us to have mercy on him, at which
        time we will bring the device to the bar and crown thee for
        a finder of madmen. But see, but see!

        Enter SIR ANDREW

FABIAN
        More matter for a May morning.

SIR ANDREW
        (presenting a paper) Here's the challenge, read it. Warrant
130   there's vinegar and pepper in 't.

FABIAN
        Is 't so saucy?

SIR ANDREW
        Ay, is 't, I warrant him. Do but read.

SIR TOBY BELCH
Is it possible?

FABIAN
If this were a play, I'd complain it was unrealistic.

SIR TOBY BELCH
He's really taken this prank to heart. He's playing the role perfectly.

MARIA
No, follow him now, before he divulges the prank and ruins everything.

FABIAN
Wow, we're really going to drive him crazy.

MARIA
The house will be so much quieter.

SIR TOBY BELCH
Come on, let's put him in a dark room and tie him up. My niece already thinks he's insane. We can go on like this, punishing him and having some fun, until we're tired of it. Then we can take mercy on him and let him out, and talk about how well the joke went. We'll also worship you for setting up this trick. Let's do it, let's do it!

SIR ANDREW enters.

FABIAN
Here's more insanity for us.

SIR ANDREW
(presenting them a piece of paper) Here's the challenge, read it. It's bursting with fighting words.

FABIAN
Is it that aggressive?

SIR ANDREW
Yes, it is, I think. Just read it.

SIR TOBY BELCH
Give me. *(reads)* "Youth, whatsoever thou art, thou art but a scurvy fellow."

FABIAN
135   Good, and valiant.

SIR TOBY BELCH
(reads) "Wonder not, nor admire not in thy mind, why I do call thee so, for I will show thee no reason for 't."

FABIAN
A good note, that keeps you from the blow of the law.

SIR TOBY BELCH
(reads) "Thou comest to the lady Olivia, and in my sight
140   she uses thee kindly. But thou liest in thy throat. That is not the matter I challenge thee for."

FABIAN
Very brief, and to exceeding good sense—less.

SIR TOBY BELCH
(reads) "I will waylay thee going home, where if it be thy chance to kill me—"

FABIAN
145   Good.

SIR TOBY BELCH
(reads) "Thou killest me like a rogue and a villain."

FABIAN
Still you keep o' the windy side of the law. Good.

SIR TOBY BELCH
(reads) "Fare thee well, and God have mercy upon one of our souls. He may have mercy upon mine, but my hope is
150   better, and so look to thyself. Thy friend, as thou usest him, and thy sworn enemy,
                    Andrew Aguecheek"

SIR TOBY BELCH

Give it to me. *(he reads)* "Young man, whatever you are, you're a real scum bucket."

FABIAN

Nice. Very courageous.

SIR TOBY BELCH

(reading) "Don't even ask why I call you that, because I won't give you any explanation."

FABIAN

That's a good thing to put in—it keeps you from getting in trouble with the law.

SIR TOBY BELCH

(reading) "You come to see the lady Olivia, and she's kind to you. But you're a complete liar. That's not why I'm challenging you to a duel."

FABIAN

Nice and short and full of good sense—or should I say nonsense?

SIR TOBY BELCH

(reading) "I'll ambush you on your way home, and if you're lucky enough to kill me—"

FABIAN

Good.

SIR TOBY BELCH

(reading) "You'll be killing me like a common criminal, a mugger."

FABIAN

You still haven't said anything incriminating. Good.

SIR TOBY BELCH

(reading) "Good luck, and may God have mercy on one of our souls. He may have mercy upon mine. But I have a better chance of surviving, so watch out. Signed, your friend, if you treat him right, and your sworn enemy,

Andrew Aguecheek"

If this letter move him not, his legs cannot. I'll give 't him.

MARIA
You may have very fit occasion for 't. He is now in some
155   commerce with my lady and will by and by depart.

SIR TOBY BELCH
Go, Sir Andrew. Scout me for him at the corner the orchard
like a bum-baily. So soon as ever thou seest him, draw, and
as thou drawest, swear horrible, for it comes to pass oft that
a terrible oath, with a swaggering accent sharply twanged
160   off, gives manhood more approbation than ever proof itself
would have earned him. Away!

SIR ANDREW
Nay, let me alone for swearing.

Exit

SIR TOBY BELCH
Now will not I deliver his letter, for the behavior of the
young gentleman gives him out to be of good capacity and
165   breeding. His employment between his lord and my niece
confirms no less. Therefore this letter, being so excellently
ignorant, will breed no terror in the youth. He will find it
comes from a clodpole. But, sir, I will deliver his challenge
by word of mouth, set upon Aguecheek a notable report of
170   valor, and drive the gentleman (as I know his youth will
aptly receive it) into a most hideous opinion of his rage,
skill, fury, and impetuosity. This will so fright them both
that they will kill one another by the look, like cockatrices.

Enter OLIVIA, *with* VIOLA

If this letter doesn't make him fight, I don't know what will. I'll give it to him.

MARIA

You might have a great opportunity to give it to him right now. He's conducting some business with my lady, and sooner or later he'll leave.

SIR TOBY BELCH

Go, Sir Andrew. Look out for him in the corner of the orchard as if you were a sheriff's deputy. As soon as you see him, draw your sword, and as you draw it, start swearing horribly. Sometimes a terrible swear word, like a well-shot arrow, makes you look more brave and manly than getting in a fight would. Now go!

SIR ANDREW

Don't worry about me not swearing enough.

SIR ANDREW exits.

SIR TOBY BELCH

I won't deliver this letter. The young gentleman's behavior shows that he's sensible and has good manners. The fact that he serves as a go-between for his lord and my niece Olivia confirms this. So this letter, which is so incredibly stupid and ignorant, isn't going to scare him at all. He'll just think an idiot wrote it. But I'll deliver Sir Andrew's challenge by word of mouth, describing Sir Andrew as courageous in battle and convincing the young gentleman that Sir Andrew is furious, impetuous, and a skilled fighter (he'll believe me because he's young). This will make them both so afraid that they'll kill each other just by looking at each other.

OLIVIA enters with VIOLA.

FABIAN

Here he comes with your niece. Give them way till he take
175   leave, and presently after him.

SIR TOBY BELCH

I will meditate the while upon some horrid message for a
challenge.

Exeunt SIR TOBY BELCH, FABIAN, *and* MARIA

OLIVIA

I have said too much unto a heart of stone
And laid mine honor too unchary on 't.
180   There's something in me that reproves my fault,
But such a headstrong potent fault it is
That it but mocks reproof.

VIOLA

With the same 'havior that your passion bears
Goes on my master's grief.

OLIVIA

185   Here, wear this jewel for me. 'Tis my picture.
Refuse it not. It hath no tongue to vex you.
And I beseech you come again tomorrow.
What shall you ask of me that I'll deny,
That honor, saved, may upon asking give?

VIOLA

190   Nothing but this: your true love for my master.

OLIVIA

How with mine honor may I give him that
Which I have given to you?

VIOLA

I will acquit you.

OLIVIA

Well, come again tomorrow. Fare thee well.
195   A fiend like thee might bear my soul to hell.

FABIAN

Here comes the messenger with your niece. Leave them alone until he sets off home, and then follow him.

SIR TOBY BELCH

Meanwhile, I'll think of some horrible way to phrase the challenge.

SIR TOBY BELCH, FABIAN, and MARIA exit.

OLIVIA

I've said too much to someone with a heart of stone. I've foolishly jeopardized my honor and reputation. I hate myself for behaving that way, but I just had to, and no criticism could have stopped me.

VIOLA

My lord acts just as crazy with love as you do.

OLIVIA

Here, take this piece of jewelry. There's a picture of me inside. Don't refuse it. It won't annoy you like me, because it doesn't have a voice. And I beg you, please come here again tomorrow. What could you possibly ask of me that I wouldn't give you, as long as it didn't damage my honor and self-respect?

VIOLA

Nothing, except your true love for my lord.

OLIVIA

How could I honorably give him what I've already given you?

VIOLA

I'll give it back to you.

OLIVIA

Just come again tomorrow. Good-bye. A devil like you could lead me to hell.

Exit

Enter SIR TOBY BELCH *and* FABIAN

SIR TOBY BELCH
Gentleman, God save thee.

VIOLA
And you, sir.

SIR TOBY BELCH
That defense thou hast, betake thee to 't. Of what nature the wrongs are thou hast done him, I know not, but thy 200 intercepter, full of despite, bloody as the hunter, attends thee at the orchard end. Dismount thy tuck, be yare in thy preparation, for thy assailant is quick, skillful and deadly.

VIOLA
You mistake, sir. I am sure no man hath any quarrel to me. My remembrance is very free and clear from any image of 205 offense done to any man.

SIR TOBY BELCH
You'll find it otherwise, I assure you. Therefore, if you hold your life at any price, betake you to your guard, for your opposite hath in him what youth, strength, skill, and wrath can furnish man withal.

VIOLA
210 I pray you, sir, what is he?

SIR TOBY BELCH
He is knight, dubbed with unhatched rapier and on carpet consideration, but he is a devil in private brawl. Souls and bodies hath he divorced three, and his incensement at this moment is so implacable that satisfaction can be none but 215 by pangs of death and sepulchre. Hob, nob, is his word. "Give 't or take 't."

OLIVIA *exits.*

SIR TOBY BELCH *and* FABIAN *enter.*

SIR TOBY BELCH

Hello, sir.

VIOLA

Hello to you.

SIR TOBY BELCH

You'd better think up a way to defend yourself. I don't know what you've done to upset him, but someone has challenged you to a duel. He's riled up and blood-thirsty, and he's waiting for you at the back of the orchard. Draw your sword and get on your toes, because your assailant is quick, skillful, and deadly.

VIOLA

There must be some mistake, sir. I'm sure nobody would have any reason to fight with me. I can't remember anything I've ever done to offend anyone.

SIR TOBY BELCH

You're wrong about that, I assure you. So if you value your life at all, be on your guard. Your opponent has enough youth, strength, skill, and anger to outfight anyone.

VIOLA

But who is this person, sir?

SIR TOBY BELCH

He's a knight. He was made a knight because of his court connections, but when he's fighting a civilian he's a real monster. He's killed three people, and he's so furious right now that the only thing that will satisfy him is seeing you die. "Fight to the death" is his motto.

VIOLA

I'll go back inside and ask the lady for some kind of escort. I'm not a fighter. I've heard of men who pick

VIOLA

> I will return again into the house and desire some conduct
> of the lady. I am no fighter. I have heard of some kind of men
> that put quarrels purposely on others, to taste their valor.
> 220 Belike this is a man of that quirk.

SIR TOBY BELCH

> Sir, no. His indignation derives itself out of a very
> competent injury. Therefore get you on and give him his
> desire. Back you shall not to the house, unless you
> undertake that with me which with as much safety you
> 225 might answer him. Therefore on, or strip your sword stark
> naked, for meddle you must, that's certain, or forswear to
> wear iron about you.

VIOLA

> This is as uncivil as strange. I beseech you, do me this
> courteous office, as to know of the knight what my offense
> 230 to him is. It is something of my negligence, nothing of my
> purpose.

SIR TOBY BELCH

> I will do so. Signior Fabian, stay you by this gentleman till
> my return.

> *Exit*

VIOLA

> Pray you, sir, do you know of this matter?

FABIAN

> 235 I know the knight is incensed against you, even to a mortal
> arbitrament, but nothing of the circumstance more.

VIOLA

> I beseech you, what manner of man is he?

FABIAN

> Nothing of that wonderful promise, to read him by his
> form, as you are like to find him in the proof of his valor. He
> 240 is, indeed, sir, the most skillful, bloody, and fatal opposite

fights with other people on purpose, just to see how brave they are. This man is probably like that.

SIR TOBY BELCH

No, sir. He's furious because you insulted him, and he has a right to satisfaction. So go out there and give him what he wants. You can't go back into the house unless you want to fight with me—and if you're willing to do that, you might as well just go and fight with him. So go to the orchard, or take out your sword right now. You're going to have to fight one way or another, there's no doubt about that, or else you'll have to stop wearing a sword and claiming to be a gentleman.

VIOLA

This is as rude as it is strange. Please, do me this one favor: find out what I've done to offend this knight. It must be something I did accidentally.

SIR TOBY BELCH

I will do so. Mr. Fabian, stay with this gentleman until I come back.

SIR TOBY exits.

VIOLA

Excuse me, sir, do you know anything about this?

FABIAN

I know the knight is furious with you, so much that he's willing to fight you to the death, but I don't know anything else about it.

VIOLA

What kind of man is he?

FABIAN

He's not much to look at, but he's very brave in battle. He really is the most skillful, bloodthirsty, and dan-

that you could possibly have found in any part of Illyria.
Will you walk towards him? I will make your peace with
him if I can.

VIOLA

I shall be much bound to you for 't. I am one that had rather
245   go with sir priest than sir knight. I care not who knows so
much of my mettle.

Exeunt

Enter SIR TOBY BELCH, *with* SIR ANDREW

SIR TOBY BELCH

Why, man, he's a very devil. I have not seen such a firago.
I had a pass with him, rapier, scabbard, and all, and he gives
me the stuck-in with such a mortal motion, that it is
250   inevitable. And on the answer, he pays you as surely as your
feet hit the ground they step on. They say he has been
fencer to the Sophy.

SIR ANDREW

Pox on 't! I'll not meddle with him.

SIR TOBY BELCH

Ay, but he will not now be pacified. Fabian can scarce hold
255   him yonder.

SIR ANDREW

Plague on 't, an I thought he had been valiant and so
cunning in fence, I'd have seen him damned ere I'd have
challenged him. Let him let the matter slip, and I'll give
him my horse, gray Capilet.

SIR TOBY BELCH

260   I'll make the motion. Stand here, make a good show on 't.
This shall end without the perdition of souls. *(aside)* Marry,
I'll ride your horse as well as I ride you.

Enter FABIAN *and* VIOLA

gerous opponent you can find in Illyria. Do you want
to go see him? I'll try to calm him down for you if I can.

VIOLA

I'd be very grateful to you if you did. I'm much more
of a religious type than a fighter, and I don't care who
knows it.

They exit.

SIR TOBY BELCH *enters with* SIR ANDREW.

SIR TOBY BELCH

Wow, he's a real devil. I've never seen such a monster.
I had a round with him, and his sword thrust is so
deadly that you can't even duck out of the way. And
when he strikes back at you, he'll hit you as sure as
you're standing there. They say he used to fence for
the shah of Persia.

SIR ANDREW

That's it! I won't mess with him.

SIR TOBY BELCH

Yes, but now there's no way to calm him down. Fabian
can hardly control him over there.

SIR ANDREW

Darn it, if I'd guessed he was so brave and such a good
swordsman, I never would have challenged him. I'll
give him my gray horse Capilet if he forgets the whole
thing.

SIR TOBY BELCH

I'll give it a try. Stay right here and try to look good.
This may end without anyone getting killed. *(to himself)* I'll ride your horse just like I ride you.

FABIAN *and* VIOLA *enter.*

(to FABIAN*)* I have his horse to take up the quarrel. I have
persuaded him the youth's a devil.

FABIAN
265   He is as horribly conceited of him, and pants and looks pale,
as if a bear were at his heels.

SIR TOBY BELCH
(to VIOLA*)* There's no remedy, sir; he will fight with you for
's oath sake. Marry, he hath better bethought him of his
quarrel, and he finds that now scarce to be worth talking of.
270   Therefore, draw for the supportance of his vow. He protests
he will not hurt you.

VIOLA
(aside) Pray God defend me! A little thing would make me
tell them how much I lack of a man.

FABIAN
Give ground, if you see him furious.

SIR TOBY BELCH
275   Come, Sir Andrew, there's no remedy. The gentleman will,
for his honor's sake, have one bout with you. He cannot by
the duello avoid it. But he has promised me, as he is a
gentleman and a soldier, he will not hurt you. Come on,
to 't.

SIR ANDREW
280   Pray God, he keep his oath!

VIOLA
I do assure you, 'tis against my will.

They draw swords
Enter ANTONIO

ANTONIO
Put up your sword. If this young gentleman
Have done offence, I take the fault on me.
If you offend him, I for him defy you.

(to FABIAN*)* He's given me his horse to try to avoid the fight—I've persuaded him that the young man is a fighting machine.

FABIAN

He's just as terrified of Sir Andrew. He's pale and hyperventilating, as if a bear were chasing him.

SIR TOBY BELCH

(to VIOLA*)* There's nothing you can do about it, sir. He insists on fighting with you because he swore he would. But he's thought over his reason for challenging you to fight, and he realizes it's so insignificant that it's not worth thinking about. So draw your sword so he can carry out his vow. He promises not to hurt you.

VIOLA

(to herself) God help me! If anything happens I'm going to have to tell them exactly how unmanly I am.

FABIAN

Back off if he seems really furious.

SIR TOBY BELCH

Come on, Sir Andrew, there's nothing you can do about it. The gentleman insists on fighting a round with you, for the sake of his honor. The rules of dueling say he has to. But as a gentleman and a soldier he's promised me he won't hurt you. Come on, get ready.

SIR ANDREW

I hope to God he keeps his promise!

VIOLA

I swear to you, I don't want to be doing this.

They draw their swords. ANTONIO *enters.*

ANTONIO

Put your sword away. If this young gentleman has offended you, I'll take the blame for it. If you've offended him, I'll fight you.

SIR TOBY BELCH

285   You, sir? Why, what are you?

ANTONIO

            One, sir, that for his love dares yet do more
            Than you have heard him brag to you he will.

SIR TOBY BELCH

            Nay, if you be an undertaker, I am for you.

            They draw swords
            Enter **OFFICERS**

FABIAN

            O good Sir Toby, hold! Here come the officers.

SIR TOBY BELCH

290   *(to* **ANTONIO***)* I'll be with you anon.

VIOLA

            (to **ANDREW***)* Pray, sir, put your sword up, if you please.

SIR ANDREW

            Marry, will I, sir. And for that I promised you, I'll be as
            good as my word. He will bear you easily and reins well.

FIRST OFFICER

            This is the man. Do thy office.

SECOND OFFICER

295   Antonio, I arrest thee at the suit of Count Orsino.

ANTONIO

            You do mistake me, sir.

FIRST OFFICER

            No, sir, no jot. I know your favor well,
            Though now you have no sea-cap on your head.—
            Take him away. He knows I know him well.

ANTONIO

300   I must obey. *(to* **VIOLA***)* This comes with seeking you:
            But there's no remedy. I shall answer it.

SIR TOBY BELCH

You, sir? Who are you?

ANTONIO

I'm just a good friend of his. In fact, I'd do even more to him than what you've heard him promise to do.

SIR TOBY BELCH

If you're someone who gets into fights, I'll fight with you.

They draw their swords. OFFICERS *enter.*

FABIAN

Oh, Sir Toby, stop! The police are here.

SIR TOBY BELCH

(to ANTONIO*)* I'll be back for you soon.

VIOLA

(to ANDREW*)* Please, sir, put away your sword. Please.

SIR ANDREW

I certainly will, sir. And as for what I promised to you, I'm as good as my word. You can ride him easily, and he responds well when you pull the reins.

FIRST OFFICER

This is the man. Do your job.

SECOND OFFICER

Antonio, you're under arrest on the orders of Count Orsino.

ANTONIO

You must be mistaking me for someone else, sir.

FIRST OFFICER

No, sir, not at all. I recognize your face perfectly, even without a sailor's cap on your head.—Take him away. He knows I recognize him.

ANTONIO

I have to obey. *(to* VIOLA*)* This has happened because I came looking for you, but there's nothing I can do

What will you do, now my necessity
Makes me to ask you for my purse? It grieves me
Much more for what I cannot do for you
305   Than what befalls myself. You stand amazed,
But be of comfort.

SECOND OFFICER
                    Come, sir, away.

ANTONIO
(to VIOLA*)* I must entreat of you some of that money.

VIOLA
What money, sir?
For the fair kindness you have showed me here,
310   And part being prompted by your present trouble,
Out of my lean and low ability
I'll lend you something. My having is not much.
I'll make division of my present with you.
Hold, there's half my coffer. *(offering him money)*

ANTONIO
                 Will you deny me now?
315   Is 't possible that my deserts to you
Can lack persuasion? Do not tempt my misery,
Lest that it make me so unsound a man
As to upbraid you with those kindnesses
That I have done for you.

VIOLA
                 I know of none,
320   Nor know I you by voice or any feature.
I hate ingratitude more in a man
Than lying, vainness, babbling, drunkenness,
Or any taint of vice whose strong corruption
Inhabits our frail blood—

ANTONIO
                O heavens themselves!

SECOND OFFICER
325   Come, sir, I pray you, go.

about it now. I'll take what's coming to me. But what'll you do now that I have to ask you for my purse back? I'm more upset about not being able to help you than I am about what's going to happen to me. You look so confused. Don't worry about me.

SECOND OFFICER

Come on, sir, let's go.

ANTONIO

(to VIOLA*)* Really, I must ask you for some of that money.

VIOLA

What money, sir? I feel sorry for you in this situation, and I want to thank you for the kindness you've shown me here, so I'll lend you some of my money, though I don't have much. I'll give you half of everything I have right now. Take this. It's half of all my money. *(she offers him money)*

ANTONIO

Are you really going to pretend you don't know me now? After everything I've done for you, you're refusing to help me? Don't make me more miserable than I am. I might do something really weak and unmanly, like listing the kind things I've done for you.

VIOLA

I don't know any kind things you've done for me, and I don't recognize your voice or your face. I hate an ungrateful man more than I hate lying, vanity, babbling, drunkenness, or any other vice that we feeble human beings are susceptible to.—

ANTONIO

Oh, my God!

SECOND OFFICER

Come on, sir, please. Let's go.

ANTONIO
Let me speak a little. This youth that you see here
I snatched one half out of the jaws of death,
Relieved him with such sanctity of love,
And to his image, which methought did promise
330   Most venerable worth, did I devotion.

FIRST OFFICER
What's that to us? The time goes by. Away!

ANTONIO
But oh, how vile an idol proves this god!
Thou hast, Sebastian, done good feature shame.
In nature there's no blemish but the mind.
335   None can be called deformed but the unkind.
Virtue is beauty, but the beauteous evil
Are empty trunks o'erflourished by the devil.

FIRST OFFICER
The man grows mad. Away with him. Come, come, sir.

ANTONIO
Lead me on.

Exit with OFFICERS

VIOLA
340   Methinks his words do from such passion fly,
That he believes himself. So do not I.
Prove true, imagination, oh, prove true,
That I, dear brother, be now ta'en for you!

SIR TOBY BELCH
Come hither, knight. Come hither, Fabian. We'll whisper
345   o'er a couplet or two of most sage saws.

VIOLA
He named Sebastian. I my brother know
Yet living in my glass. Even such and so
In favor was my brother, and he went

ANTONIO

> No, I've got something to say. I saved this young man's life when he was half-dead, and nursed him back to health lovingly and tenderly. I devoted myself to him, since he looked noble and good.

FIRST OFFICER

> Why should we care? Time's passing. Let's go!

ANTONIO

> But oh, what a deceiver he turned out to be! You don't live up to your good looks, Sebastian. You look good but you're bad on the inside, where it counts, since the only real flaws in nature are in a person's mind and soul. Only really cruel people can be called deformed. Virtue is beauty, but someone beautiful and wicked is like an empty box decorated by the devil.

FIRST OFFICER

> The man's going crazy. Take him away. Come on, sir. Come on.

ANTONIO

> Take me.

He exits with the OFFICERS.

VIOLA

> He was so angry I feel he must really believe what he was saying. I don't believe it. Yet I wish I could. Oh, please be true, please let it be that this man has mistaken me for you, my dear brother!

SIR TOBY BELCH

> Come here, Sir Andrew. You too, Fabian. We've got some words of wisdom to mull over.

VIOLA

> He called me Sebastian. I know my brother's still alive in a sense, since I see him whenever I look in the mirror. My brother looked like me, and he dressed the same way that I'm dressed now—in the same colors,

Still in this fashion, color, ornament,
350   For him I imitate. Oh, if it prove,
Tempests are kind and salt waves fresh in love!

Exit

SIR TOBY BELCH
A very dishonest paltry boy, and more a coward than a hare.
His dishonesty appears in leaving his friend here in
necessity and denying him. And for his cowardship, ask
355   Fabian.

FABIAN
A coward, a most devout coward, religious in it.

SIR ANDREW
'Slid, I'll after him again and beat him.

SIR TOBY BELCH
Do, cuff him soundly, but never draw thy sword.

SIR ANDREW
An I do not—

FABIAN
360   Come, let's see the event.

SIR TOBY BELCH
I dare lay any money 'twill be nothing yet.

Exeunt

with the same accessories. Oh, if it turns out to be true that he survived, then that storm was kind, and the ocean was full of love!

VIOLA exits.

SIR TOBY BELCH

He's a very dishonest, puny boy, and more cowardly than a rabbit. He abandoned his friend here in an emergency, and even pretended he didn't know him. That shows he's dishonest. As for his cowardliness, ask Fabian.

FABIAN

He's a coward, a total coward. He's religiously devoted to his cowardice.

SIR ANDREW

By God, I'll go after him again and beat him up.

SIR TOBY BELCH

Please do. Beat him up well, but don't draw your sword.

SIR ANDREW

I swear I will—

FABIAN

Come on, let's go see what happens.

SIR TOBY BELCH

I'll bet anything you like that nothing will happen, once again.

They all exit.

ACT FOUR

SCENE 1

Enter SEBASTIAN *and* FOOL

FOOL

Will you make me believe that I am not sent for you?

SEBASTIAN

Go to, go to, thou art a foolish fellow. Let me be clear of thee.

FOOL

Well held out, i' faith. No, I do not know you, nor I am not
5   sent to you by my lady, to bid you come speak with her, nor
your name is not Master Cesario, nor this is not my nose
neither. Nothing that is so is so.

SEBASTIAN

I prithee, vent thy folly somewhere else. Thou know'st not
me.

FOOL

10   Vent my folly? He has heard that word of some great man
and now applies it to a fool. Vent my folly! I am afraid this
great lubber, the world, will prove a cockney. I prithee now,
ungird thy strangeness and tell me what I shall vent to my
lady. Shall I vent to her that thou art coming?

SEBASTIAN

15   I prithee, foolish Greek, depart from me. There's money for
thee. *(giving money)* If you tarry longer, I shall give worse
payment.

FOOL

By my troth, thou hast an open hand. These wise men that
give fools money get themselves a good report—after
20   fourteen years' purchase.

ACT FOUR

SCENE 1

SEBASTIAN *and the* FOOL *enter.*

FOOL

Are you trying to tell me that I wasn't sent to get you?

SEBASTIAN

Oh, who cares, you're acting like a fool. Leave me alone.

FOOL

Good for you, holding out on me like this! No, I don't know you, and my lady didn't send me to get you, and I'm not supposed to tell you to come speak with her, and your name is not Master Cesario, and this is not my nose, either. Nothing is what it is.

SEBASTIAN

Oh please, go somewhere else to blab your nonsense. You don't know me.

FOOL

Blab my nonsense? He must've heard that phrase describing some great man and now he's using it on a jester. Blab my nonsense! What an idiotic place this world is. Now please stop being so strange and tell me what exactly I should blab to my lady. Should I blab to her that you're coming?

SEBASTIAN

Please, fool, go away. Here's money for you. *(giving him money)* If you stay any longer, I'll give you something worse.

FOOL

Well, well. You're a generous man. Wise men who give fools money might get a good reputation—if they keep up regular payments for fourteen years.

Enter SIR ANDREW, SIR TOBY BELCH, *and* FABIAN

SIR ANDREW
(to SEBASTIAN*)* Now, sir, have I met you again? There's for
you.

SIR ANDREW *strikes* SEBASTIAN

SEBASTIAN
(returning the blow) Why, there's for thee, and there, and
there. Are all the people mad?

SIR TOBY BELCH
25   Hold, sir, or I'll throw your dagger o'er the house.

FOOL
(aside) This will I tell my lady straight. I would not be in
some of your coats for two pence.

Exit

SIR TOBY BELCH
(seizing SEBASTIAN*)* Come on, sir, hold!

SIR ANDREW
Nay, let him alone. I'll go another way to work with him. I'll
30   have an action of battery against him if there be any law in
Illyria. Though I struck him first, yet it's no matter for that.

SEBASTIAN
(to SIR TOBY BELCH*)* Let go thy hand.

SIR TOBY BELCH
Come, sir, I will not let you go. Come, my young soldier,
put up your iron. You are well fleshed. Come on.

SEBASTIAN
35   I will be free from thee.

SEBASTIAN *pulls free and draws his sword*

SIR ANDREW, SIR TOBY BELCH, *and* FABIAN *enter.*

SIR ANDREW

> Well, sir, we meet again? Take that.

SIR ANDREW *hits* SEBASTIAN.

SEBASTIAN

> *(returning the blow)* Well, then, take that, and that, and that. Is everyone here insane?

SIR TOBY BELCH

> Stop right now or I'll throw your dagger over the roof.

FOOL

> *(to himself)* I'm going to tell my lady about this right away. I wouldn't be in any of your shoes if you paid me.

FOOL *exits.*

SIR TOBY BELCH

> *(grabbing* SEBASTIAN*)* Come on, sir, stop!

SIR ANDREW

> No, leave him alone. I'll get back at him another way. I'll sue him for assault and battery, if there's any justice in Illyria. It doesn't matter that I hit him first.

SEBASTIAN

> *(to* SIR TOBY BELCH*)* Let me go.

SIR TOBY BELCH

> No, sir, I won't let you go. Come on, put your sword away, my little soldier. You're awfully eager to fight. Come on.

SEBASTIAN

> I'll get free of you.

SEBASTIAN *pulls free and draws his sword.*

What wouldst thou now? If thou darest tempt me further,
draw thy sword.

SIR TOBY BELCH
What, what? Nay, then I must have an ounce or two of this
malapert blood from you.

SIR TOBY BELCH draws his sword
Enter OLIVIA

OLIVIA
40   Hold, Toby! On thy life I charge thee, hold!

SIR TOBY BELCH
Madam!

OLIVIA
Will it be ever thus? Ungracious wretch,
Fit for the mountains and the barbarous caves,
Where manners ne'er were preach'd! Out of my sight!—
45   Be not offended, dear Cesario.—
Rudesby, be gone!

Exeunt SIR TOBY BELCH, SIR ANDREW, and FABIAN

I prithee, gentle friend,
Let thy fair wisdom, not thy passion, sway
In this uncivil and unjust extent
Against thy peace. Go with me to my house,
50   And hear thou there how many fruitless pranks
This ruffian hath botched up, that thou thereby
Mayst smile at this. Thou shalt not choose but go.
Do not deny. Beshrew his soul for me!
He started one poor heart of mine in thee.

SEBASTIAN
55   (*aside*) What relish is in this? How runs the stream?
Or I am mad, or else this is a dream.
Let fancy still my sense in Lethe steep.

What are you going to do now? If you insist on trying my patience any further, then take out your sword right now.

SIR TOBY BELCH

What? No. Because then I'd have to shed an ounce or two of your impudent blood.

SIR TOBY BELCH *draws his sword.* OLIVIA *enters.*

OLIVIA

Stop, Sir Toby! I order you to stop!

SIR TOBY BELCH

Madam!

OLIVIA

Are you always going to be like this? You're an ungrateful slob who's only fit to live in the mountains, in caves far from civilized people where you won't ever need good manners! Get out of my sight!—Dear Cesario, please don't be offended.—Get out of here, you barbarian!

SIR TOBY BELCH, SIR ANDREW, *and* FABIAN *exit.*

Oh, my dear friend, please don't get too upset by these rude people who bothered you. Come with me to my house. I'll tell you about all the pointless, clumsy pranks this thug uncle of mine has come up with, so that you can laugh at this one. You have to come with me. Please don't say no. Damn that Toby! He made my heart leap for you.

SEBASTIAN

(to himself) What does this mean? Where is this all going? Either I'm insane or this is a dream. I hope

        If it be thus to dream, still let me sleep!

OLIVIA
        Nay, come, I prithee. Would thou'dst be ruled by me!

SEBASTIAN
60   Madam, I will.

OLIVIA
        Oh, say so, and so be!

                                                Exeunt

these delusions continue. If this is a dream, let me keep on sleeping!

OLIVIA

Come with me, please. I wish you'd do what I ask!

SEBASTIAN

Madam, I will.

OLIVIA

Oh, say it, and mean it!

They exit.

ACT 4, SCENE 2

Enter MARIA *and* FOOL

MARIA

Nay, I prithee, put on this gown and this beard. Make him
believe thou art Sir Topas the curate. Do it quickly. I'll call
Sir Toby the whilst.

Exit

FOOL

Well, I'll put it on, and I will dissemble myself in 't, and I
5   would I were the first that ever dissembled in such a gown.

FOOL *puts on gown and beard*

I am not tall enough to become the function well, nor lean
enough to be thought a good student, but to be said an
honest man and a good housekeeper goes as fairly as to say
a careful man and a great scholar. The competitors enter.

Enter SIR TOBY BELCH *and* MARIA

SIR TOBY BELCH

10   Jove bless thee, master Parson.

FOOL

Bonos dies, Sir Toby. For, as the old hermit of Prague, that
never saw pen and ink, very wittily said to a niece of King
Gorboduc, "That that is is." So I, being Master Parson, am
Master Parson. For, what is "that" but "that," and "is" but
15   "is"?

SIR TOBY BELCH

To him, Sir Topas.

ACT 4, SCENE 2

MARIA *and the* FOOL *enter.*

MARIA

> No, I'm telling you, put on this robe and beard. Make him think you're Sir Topas the priest. Be quick. Meanwhile, I'll get Sir Toby.

> MARIA *exits.*

FOOL

> Well, I'll put it on and disguise myself. I wish I were the first person who ever told lies in a priest's robe.

> *The* FOOL *puts on the robe and beard.*

> I'm not tall enough to make a believable priest, or skinny enough to look like a good student. But if you're an honest man and a good host, that's almost as good as being moral and studious. Here come the conspirators.

> SIR TOBY BELCH *and* MARIA *enter.*

SIR TOBY BELCH
> God bless you, Mr. Priest.

FOOL

The fool is saying hello in an imitation of Latin.

> *Bonos dies*, Sir Toby. As the old hermit of Prague, who couldn't read or write, said very wittily to a niece of King Gorboduc, "Whatever is, is." So since I'm Mr. Priest, I'm Mr. Priest. Because isn't "that" "that," and isn't "is" "is"?

SIR TOBY BELCH
> Go to him, Sir Topas.

FOOL

(disguising his voice) What ho, I say! Peace in this prison!

SIR TOBY BELCH

The knave counterfeits well. A good knave.

MALVOLIO

(from within) Who calls there?

FOOL

20   Sir Topas the curate, who comes to visit Malvolio the
lunatic.

MALVOLIO

Sir Topas, Sir Topas, good Sir Topas, go to my lady—

FOOL

Out, hyperbolical fiend! How vexest thou this man! Talkest
thou nothing but of ladies?

SIR TOBY BELCH

25   *(aside)* Well said, Master Parson.

MALVOLIO

Sir Topas, never was man thus wronged. Good Sir Topas,
do not think I am mad. They have laid me here in hideous
darkness.

FOOL

Fie, thou dishonest Satan! I call thee by the most modest
30   terms, for I am one of those gentle ones that will use the
devil himself with courtesy. Sayest thou that house is dark?

MALVOLIO

As hell, Sir Topas.

FOOL

Why, it hath bay windows transparent as barricadoes, and
the clerestories toward the south-north are as lustrous as
35   ebony. And yet complainest thou of obstruction?

MALVOLIO

I am not mad, Sir Topas. I say to you this house is dark.

FOOL

(disguising his voice) Quiet down in this prison!

SIR TOBY BELCH

The fool's a good actor. A good fool.

MALVOLIO

(offstage) Who's shouting?

FOOL

I'm Sir Topas the priest. I've come to visit Malvolio the lunatic.

MALVOLIO

Sir Topas, Sir Topas, good Sir Topas, please go find my lady Olivia—

FOOL

Get out, demon! Why are you bothering this poor man! Can't you talk about anything besides ladies?

SIR TOBY BELCH

(to himself) Well said, Mr. Priest.

MALVOLIO

Sir Topas, nobody's ever been as badly treated as I've been. Good Sir Topas, don't believe I'm insane, They've shut me up here in horrible darkness.

FOOL

You should be ashamed of yourself, Satan, you liar! I'm being gentle with you, because I'm one of those good-hearted people who are polite to the devil himself. You call this house dark?

MALVOLIO

Dark as hell, Sir Topas.

FOOL

But it has bay windows that are as transparent as stone walls, and the upper windows facing south-north are as clear as coal. But you're still complaining of darkness and a bad view?

MALVOLIO

I'm not insane, Sir Topas. I'm telling you, this house is dark.

FOOL

Madman, thou errest. I say, there is no darkness but
ignorance, in which thou art more puzzled than the
Egyptians in their fog.

MALVOLIO

40   I say, this house is as dark as ignorance, though ignorance
were as dark as hell. And I say, there was never man thus
abused. I am no more mad than you are. Make the trial of
it in any constant question.

FOOL

What is the opinion of Pythagoras concerning wildfowl?

MALVOLIO

45   That the soul of our grandam might haply inhabit a bird.

FOOL

What thinkest thou of his opinion?

MALVOLIO

I think nobly of the soul, and no way approve his opinion.

FOOL

Fare thee well. Remain thou still in darkness. Thou shalt
hold the opinion of Pythagoras ere I will allow of thy wits,
50   and fear to kill a woodcock lest thou dispossess the soul of
thy grandam. Fare thee well.

MALVOLIO

Sir Topas, Sir Topas!

SIR TOBY BELCH

My most exquisite Sir Topas!

FOOL

Nay, I am for all waters.

MARIA

55   Thou mightst have done this without thy beard and gown.
He sees thee not.

FOOL

> You're wrong, you madman. There's no darkness except ignorance, and you're more ignorant than the Egyptians during the plague of fog.

MALVOLIO

> I tell you, this house is as dark as ignorance. And I tell you, no man has ever been treated worse than me. I'm no more insane than you are, and I'll prove it. Ask me any commonsense question.

FOOL

> What was the philosopher Pythagoras's belief about wild birds?

MALVOLIO

> That our grandmother's soul could end up inhabiting a bird.

FOOL

> What do you think of his belief?

MALVOLIO

> I respect the soul very much, so I disagree with his belief.

FOOL

> Well then, goodbye. Stay in the dark. I'll only admit that you're sane when you agree with Pythagoras and hesitate to kill a bird because it might contain your grandmother's soul. Goodbye.

MALVOLIO

> Sir Topas, Sir Topas!

SIR TOBY BELCH

> The brilliant Sir Topas!

FOOL

> I can do anything!

MARIA

> You could've done this without your beard and gown. He couldn't see you.

SIR TOBY BELCH
> To him in thine own voice, and bring me word how thou
> findest him. I would we were well rid of this knavery. If he
> may be conveniently delivered, I would he were, for I am
> 60 now so far in offense with my niece that I cannot pursue
> with any safety this sport to the upshot. Come by and by to
> my chamber.

> *Exeunt* SIR TOBY BELCH *and* MARIA

FOOL
> *(sings in his own voice)*
> *Hey, Robin, jolly Robin,*
> *Tell me how thy lady does.*

MALVOLIO
> 65 Fool!

FOOL
> *(sings) My lady is unkind, perdy.*

MALVOLIO
> Fool!

FOOL
> *(sings) Alas, why is she so?*

MALVOLIO
> Fool, I say!

FOOL
> 70 *(sings) She loves another*—*Who calls, ha?*

MALVOLIO
> Good fool, as ever thou wilt deserve well at my hand, help
> me to a candle, and pen, ink, and paper. As I am a
> gentleman, I will live to be thankful to thee for 't.

FOOL
> Master Malvolio?

MALVOLIO
> 75 Ay, good fool.

SIR TOBY BELCH

Now talk to him in your own voice, and tell me how he is. I wish this trick would be over. If we can find a convenient way to let him go, I want to do it. I'm in so much trouble with my niece that it wouldn't be safe to let this prank go to its conclusion. Come to my room later on.

SIR TOBY BELCH and MARIA exit.

FOOL

(he sings in his own voice)
        Hey, Robin, jolly Robin,
        Tell me how your lady is.

MALVOLIO

Fool!

FOOL

(singing) My lady's mean, and that's a fact.

MALVOLIO

Fool!

FOOL

(singing) Oh, I'm sorry, why is she mean?

MALVOLIO

Fool, I say!

FOOL

(singing) She loves someone else—Who's shouting?

MALVOLIO

Good fool, good jester, I'll make it worth your while if you get me a candle, and a pen, ink and paper. You have my word as a gentleman that I'll always be grateful to you.

FOOL

Master Malvolio?

MALVOLIO

Yes, good fool.

FOOL

Alas, sir, how fell you besides your five wits?

MALVOLIO

Fool, there was never a man so notoriously abused: I am as
well in my wits, Fool, as thou art.

FOOL

But as well? Then you are mad indeed, if you be no better
80 in your wits than a fool.

MALVOLIO

They have here propertied me, keep me in darkness, send
ministers to me—asses!—and do all they can to face me out
of my wits.

FOOL

Advise you what you say. The minister is here. *(in the voice*
85 *of Sir Topas)* Malvolio, Malvolio, thy wits the heavens
restore! Endeavor thyself to sleep, and leave thy vain
bibble-babble.

MALVOLIO

Sir Topas!

FOOL

(as Sir Topas) Maintain no words with him, good fellow. *(in*
90 *his own voice)* Who, I, sir? Not I, sir. God b' wi' you , good
Sir Topas. *(as Sir Topas)* Marry, amen. *(in his own voice)* I
will, sir, I will.

MALVOLIO

Fool, fool, fool, I say!

FOOL

Alas, sir, be patient. What say you sir? I am shent for
95 speaking to you.

MALVOLIO

Good fool, help me to some light and some paper. I tell
thee, I am as well in my wits as any man in Illyria.

FOOL

Well-a-day that you were, sir.

FOOL

Poor man, how did you go insane?

MALVOLIO

Fool, no one has ever been as mistreated as I am. I'm completely sane, Fool. I'm as sane as you are.

FOOL

As sane as me? Then you really are insane, if you're no saner than a fool.

MALVOLIO

They treat me like garbage here. They keep me in darkness, and send idiotic priests to talk to me—those asses!—and do everything they can to insist I'm insane.

FOOL

Be careful what you say—the priest is here. *(in the voice of Sir Topas)* Malvolio, Malvolio, may heaven make you sane again! Try to sleep, and stop your pointless babbling.

MALVOLIO

Sir Topas!

FOOL

(as Sir Topas) Don't talk to him, my friend. *(in his own voice)* Who, me, sir? Not me, sir. God be with you, Sir Topas, goodbye. *(as Sir Topas)* Well then, amen. *(in his own voice)* Goodbye, sir.

MALVOLIO

Fool, fool, hey, fool!

FOOL

Please, sir, be quiet. What do you want to say, sir? I've just been scolded for speaking to you.

MALVOLIO

Be a nice fool and help me find a candle and some paper. I tell you, I'm as sane as any man in Illyria.

FOOL

If only you were, sir.

MALVOLIO

By this hand, I am. Good fool, some ink, paper, and light,
100   and convey what I will set down to my lady. It shall
advantage thee more than ever the bearing of letter did.

FOOL

I will help you to 't. But tell me true, are you not mad
indeed? Or do you but counterfeit?

MALVOLIO

Believe me, I am not. I tell thee true.

FOOL

105   Nay, I'll ne'er believe a madman till I see his brains. I will
fetch you light, and paper, and ink.

MALVOLIO

Fool, I'll requite it in the highest degree. I prithee, be gone.

FOOL

(sings)

> *I am gone, sir,*
> *And anon, sir,*
110   *I'll be with you again,*
> *In a trice,*
> *Like to the old Vice,*
> *Your need to sustain,*
> *Who, with dagger of lath*
115   *In his rage and his wrath,*
> *Cries "Aha," to the devil,*
> *Like a mad lad,*
> *"Pare thy nails, dad,*
> *Adieu, goodman devil."*

Exit

MALVOLIO

I swear I am. Get me some ink, paper, and a candle. I'll write a letter and you'll take it to my lady. You'll get a bigger reward than you ever got delivering a letter before.

FOOL

I'll help you. But tell me honestly, are you sure you're not insane? Or are you just pretending?

MALVOLIO

Believe me, I'm not. I'm telling the truth.

FOOL

I'll never believe a madman until I can see his brains. But I'll get you a candle and paper and ink.

MALVOLIO

Fool, I'll repay you for this favor. Please, hurry.

FOOL

(he sings)
> *I'm going now, sir, but soon*
> *I'll be with you again,*
> *To help you resist the devil,*
> *Like the sidekick in the old plays*
> *Who shakes a wooden dagger,*
> *Fumes in rage and wrath,*
> *And shouts "Whoa!" to the devil.*
> *He yells, "Trim your nails, old man.*
> *And goodbye, Satan, you peasant."*

FOOL *exits.*

ACT 4, SCENE 3

Enter SEBASTIAN

SEBASTIAN

This is the air, that is the glorious sun.
This pearl she gave me, I do feel 't and see 't,
And though 'tis wonder that enwraps me thus,
Yet 'tis not madness. Where's Antonio, then?
5   I could not find him at the Elephant.
Yet there he was, and there I found this credit,
That he did range the town to seek me out.
His counsel now might do me golden service.
For though my soul disputes well with my sense
10   That this may be some error, but no madness,
Yet doth this accident and flood of fortune
So far exceed all instance, all discourse,
That I am ready to distrust mine eyes
And wrangle with my reason that persuades me
15   To any other trust but that I am mad—
Or else the lady's mad. Yet if 'twere so,
She could not sway her house, command her followers,
Take and give back affairs and their dispatch
With such a smooth, discreet, and stable bearing
20   As I perceive she does. There's something in 't
That is deceivable. But here the lady comes.

Enter OLIVIA *and* PRIEST

ACT 4, SCENE 3

SEBASTIAN *enters.*

SEBASTIAN

This is the air, that's the glorious sun. I can feel and see this pearl she gave me. I may be dazed and confused, but I'm not insane. Where's Antonio, then? I didn't find him at the Elephant. But he'd been there before me, and they told me he'd gone out looking for me. I could really use his advice right now. I feel sure this situation is due to some mistake, and I don't think I'm crazy. But this sudden flood of good luck is so unbelievable that I'm ready to distrust my own eyes and my own rational mind when they tell me I'm not insane—maybe the lady's insane. But if that were the case, she wouldn't be able to run her house, command her servants, listen to reports, make decisions, and take care of business as smoothly as she does. There's something going on that's not what it seems. But here she comes.

OLIVIA *and a* PRIEST *enter.*

OLIVIA
(to SEBASTIAN*)*
Blame not this haste of mine. If you mean well,
Now go with me and with this holy man
Into the chantry by. There, before him
25 And underneath that consecrated roof,
Plight me the full assurance of your faith,
That my most jealous and too doubtful soul
May live at peace. He shall conceal it
Whiles you are willing it shall come to note,
30 What time we will our celebration keep
According to my birth. What do you say?

SEBASTIAN
I'll follow this good man, and go with you;
And, having sworn truth, ever will be true.

OLIVIA
Then lead the way, good father; and heavens so shine
35 That they may fairly note this act of mine.

Exeunt

OLIVIA

(to SEBASTIAN*)* Don't be angry with me for acting so quickly. If your intentions toward me are honorable, come with me and this holy man into the chapel over there, where you can soothe all my worries by making your marriage vows to me. The priest will keep it secret until you're ready to make the news public and we can throw a full marriage celebration that befits my social standing. What do you say?

SEBASTIAN

I'll follow the priest and go with you; and after I've sworn to be faithful, I'll be faithful forever.

OLIVIA

Then lead the way, father. I want the skies bright and shining to show its approval of our wedding.

They all exit.

ACT FIVE

SCENE 1

Enter FOOL *and* FABIAN

FABIAN
Now, as thou lovest me, let me see his letter.

FOOL
Good Master Fabian, grant me another request.

FABIAN
Anything.

FOOL
Do not desire to see this letter.

FABIAN
5   This is, to give a dog and in recompense desire my dog again.

Enter ORSINO, VIOLA, CURIO, *and lords*

ORSINO
Belong you to the Lady Olivia, friends?

FOOL
Ay, sir, we are some of her trappings.

ORSINO
I know thee well. How dost thou, my good fellow?

FOOL
10   Truly, sir, the better for my foes and the worse for my friends.

ORSINO
Just the contrary. The better for thy friends.

FOOL
No, sir, the worse.

ORSINO
How can that be?

ACT FIVE

SCENE 1

The FOOL *and* FABIAN *enter.*

FABIAN

If you're my friend, you'll let me see his letter.

FOOL

Dear Mr. Fabian, do me another favor first.

FABIAN

Anything.

FOOL

Don't ask to see this letter.

FABIAN

That's like giving someone a dog as a present, and then asking for the dog back in return.

ORSINO, VIOLA, CURIO, *and lords enter.*

ORSINO

My friends, are you all Lady Olivia's servants?

FOOL

Yes, sir, we're part of her entourage.

ORSINO

I know you. How are you, my friend?

FOOL

I'm better off because of my enemies, and worse off because of my friends.

ORSINO

You mean it the other way around. You're better off because of your friends.

FOOL

No, sir, worse off.

ORSINO

How can that be?

FOOL

15   Marry, sir, they praise me and make an ass of me, now my
      foes tell me plainly I am an ass. So that by my foes, sir I
      profit in the knowledge of myself, and by my friends, I am
      abused. So that, conclusions to be as kisses, if your four
      negatives make your two affirmatives, why then the worse
20   for my friends and the better for my foes.

ORSINO

      Why, this is excellent.

FOOL

      By my troth, sir, no—though it please you to be one of my
      friends.

ORSINO

      (*giving a coin*)
      Thou shalt not be the worse for me: there's gold.

FOOL

25   But that it would be double-dealing, sir, I would you could
      make it another.

ORSINO

      O, you give me ill counsel.

FOOL

      Put your grace in your pocket, sir, for this once, and let your
      flesh and blood obey it.

ORSINO

30   Well, I will be so much a sinner, to be a double-dealer.
      There's another. (*giving a coin*)

FOOL

      Primo, secundo, tertio is a good play, and the old saying is,
      the third pays for all. The triplex, sir, is a good tripping
      measure, or the bells of Saint Bennet, sir, may put you in
35   mind—one, two, three.

FOOL

Well, my friends praise me and make me look like an idiot, while my enemies tell me straightforwardly that I am an idiot. My enemies help me understand myself better, which is an advantage, and my friends help me lie about myself, which is a disadvantage. So if four negatives make two affirmatives, I'm worse off because of my friends and better off because of my foes.

ORSINO

That's excellent.

FOOL

Don't say that—unless you want to be one of my friends.

ORSINO

(he gives him a coin) You won't be worse off because of me: here's some money.

FOOL

That's a nice hand you dealt me. But if it's not double-dealing, sir, I wish you'd deal me another.

ORSINO

Oh, you're a naughty one, encouraging double-dealing.

FOOL

Ignore your virtue and nobility just this once, sir, go ahead.

ORSINO

Well, I'll commit the sin of double-dealing, and deal you a second coin. Here it is. *(he gives him another coin)*

FOOL

And maybe a third? You know, there's a game called "third time's the charm," which is fun to play, and they always say that three's a magic number. The three-beat rhythm is a good for dancing, and the church bells chime—one, two, three.

ORSINO
You can fool no more money out of me at this throw. If you
will let your lady know I am here to speak with her, and
bring her along with you, it may awake my bounty further.

FOOL
Marry, sir, lullaby to your bounty till I come again. I go, sir,
40   but I would not have you to think that my desire of having
is the sin of covetousness. But, as you say, sir, let your
bounty take a nap, I will awake it anon.

Exit

VIOLA
Here comes the man, sir, that did rescue me.

Enter ANTONIO *and* OFFICERS

ORSINO
That face of his I do remember well.
45   Yet, when I saw it last, it was besmeared
As black as Vulcan in the smoke of war.
A baubling vessel was he captain of,
For shallow draught and bulk unprizable,
With which such scathful grapple did he make
50   With the most noble bottom of our fleet,
That very envy and the tongue of loss
Cried fame and honor on him.—What's the matter?

FIRST OFFICER
Orsino, this is that Antonio
That took the *Phoenix* and her fraught from Candy,
55   And this is he that did the *Tiger* board
When your young nephew Titus lost his leg.
Here in the streets, desperate of shame and state,
In private brabble did we apprehend him.

ORSINO

You can't get any more money out of me right now. If you tell your lady I'm here to speak with her, and bring her out with you when you come back, you might make me more generous.

FOOL

Well then, sing a lullaby to your generosity: it'll nap until I come back. But don't think I'm doing this because I'm greedy. I'll be back soon to wake up your generosity.

The FOOL *exits.*

VIOLA

Here comes the man who rescued me, sir.

ANTONIO *and* OFFICERS *enter.*

ORSINO

I remember his face well. Though the last time I saw him it was black from the smoke of war. He was the captain of a flimsy boat that was practically worthless because it was so small. But with that tiny boat he fought such a fierce battle against the largest warship in our fleet that we had to admire his courage and skill even though he caused us a lot of damage.—What's going on?

FIRST OFFICER

Orsino, this is the same Antonio who took the *Phoenix* and her cargo from Crete and captured our ship the *Tiger* during the battle where your young nephew Titus lost his leg. We arrested him here for fighting in the streets. It's as if he didn't care we were on the look-out for him here.

VIOLA

> He did me kindness, sir, drew on my side,
> 60 But in conclusion put strange speech upon me.
> I know not what 'twas but distraction.

ORSINO

> Notable pirate! Thou saltwater thief,
> What foolish boldness brought thee to their mercies,
> Whom thou, in terms so bloody and so dear,
> 65 Hast made thine enemies?

ANTONIO

> Orsino, noble sir,
> Be pleased that I shake off these names you give me.
> Antonio never yet was thief or pirate,
> Though, I confess, on base and ground enough,
> Orsino's enemy. A witchcraft drew me hither.
> 70 That most ingrateful boy there by your side
> From the rude sea's enraged and foamy mouth
> Did I redeem. A wreck past hope he was.
> His life I gave him and did thereto add
> My love, without retention or restraint,
> 75 All his in dedication. For his sake
> Did I expose myself, pure for his love,
> Into the danger of this adverse town,
> Drew to defend him when he was beset,
> Where being apprehended, his false cunning,
> 80 (Not meaning to partake with me in danger)
> Taught him to face me out of his acquaintance,
> And grew a twenty-years-removed thing
> While one would wink, denied me mine own purse,
> Which I had recommended to his use
> 85 Not half an hour before.

VIOLA

> How can this be?

ORSINO

> *(to* ANTONIO*)* When came he to this town?

VIOLA

He was kind to me and took my side in the fight. But then he said strange things to me. He might be insane. I don't know what else it could be.

ORSINO

But you're a famous pirate! A master thief of the seas! What made you stupid and careless enough to come visit the people you robbed and slaughtered?

ANTONIO

Orsino, sir, please don't call me those names. I was never a thief or a pirate, though I admit I was your enemy for good reasons. I came here because someone put a spell on me. I rescued that ungrateful boy next to you from drowning. He was a wreck, almost past hope. I saved his life and gave him my love, without reservation. I dedicated myself to him. For his sake I ran the risk of revisiting this unfriendly town, and I drew my sword to defend him when he was in trouble. But when the police caught us, he was clever and treacherous enough to pretend he'd never met me before. He acted like someone who barely knew me. He refused to give me my own wallet, which I had lent him only half an hour before.

VIOLA

How is that possible?

ORSINO

(to **ANTONIO***)* When did he come to town?

ANTONIO

> Today, my lord, and for three months before,
> No interim, not a minute's vacancy,
90 > Both day and night did we keep company.

Enter OLIVIA *and attendants*

ORSINO

> Here comes the Countess. Now heaven walks on earth.
> But for thee, fellow. Fellow, thy words are madness:
> Three months this youth hath tended upon me;
> But more of that anon. *(to an officer)* Take him aside.

OLIVIA

95 > What would my lord, but that he may not have,
> Wherein Olivia may seem serviceable?
> Cesario, you do not keep promise with me.

VIOLA

> Madam?

ORSINO

> Gracious Olivia—

OLIVIA

100 > What do you say, Cesario?—Good my lord—

VIOLA

> My lord would speak. My duty hushes me.

OLIVIA

> If it be aught to the old tune, my lord,
> It is as fat and fulsome to mine ear
> As howling after music.

ORSINO

105 > Still so cruel?

OLIVIA

> Still so constant, lord.

ANTONIO

Today, my lord. And for three months before that, we spent every day and night together.

OLIVIA and attendants enter.

ORSINO

Ah, the countess is coming! An angel is walking on earth. But as for you, mister, what you're saying is insane. This young man has worked for me for three months; but more about that later. *(to an officer)* Take him away.

OLIVIA

What can I give you that you want, my lord, except the one thing you can't have? Cesario, you missed your appointment with me.

VIOLA

Madam?

ORSINO

Dearest Olivia—

OLIVIA

What do you have to say for yourself, Cesario?—My lord, please—

VIOLA

My lord wants to speak. It's my duty to be quiet.

OLIVIA

If what you have to say is anything like what you used to say, it'll be as repulsive to my ears as wild screams after beautiful music.

ORSINO

Are you still so cruel?

OLIVIA

I am still so faithful, my lord.

ORSINO
What, to perverseness? You, uncivil lady,
To whose ingrate and unauspicious altars
My soul the faithfull'st off'rings have breathed out
110   That e'er devotion tendered—what shall I do?

OLIVIA
Even what it please my lord that shall become him.

ORSINO
Why should I not, had I the heart to do it,
Like to the Egyptian thief at point of death,
Kill what I love?—A savage jealousy
115   That sometimes savors nobly. But hear me this:
Since you to nonregardance cast my faith,
And that I partly know the instrument
That screws me from my true place in your favor,
Live you the marble-breasted tyrant still.
120   But this your minion, whom I know you love,
And whom, by heaven I swear, I tender dearly,
Him will I tear out of that cruel eye
Where he sits crowned in his master's spite.
Come, boy, with me. My thoughts are ripe in mischief:
125   I'll sacrifice the lamb that I do love
To spite a raven's heart within a dove.

VIOLA
And I, most jocund, apt, and willingly,
To do you rest, a thousand deaths would die.

OLIVIA
Where goes Cesario?

VIOLA
                        After him I love
130   More than I love these eyes, more than my life,
More, by all mores, than e'er I shall love wife.
If I do feign, you witnesses above,
Punish my life for tainting of my love!

ORSINO

What, faithful to being mean and nasty? You're not polite! I breathed from my soul the most faithful offerings to your ungrateful altars that any devoted person has ever offered—what more am I supposed to do?

OLIVIA

You can do whatever you want as long as it's socially appropriate.

ORSINO

Maybe I should act like the Egyptian thief who kills the woman he loves before he dies? That kind of savage jealousy sometimes seems noble. But listen to me. Since you keep denying the love I feel for you, and since I know who's stealing my place in your heart, you can go on being cold-hearted, but I'm going to take this boy from you. He knows his master loves you. I'm doing this, even though he's dear to me, because I know you love him. Come with me, boy. I'm ready to do something extreme. I'll sacrifice this boy I care for, just to spite a beautiful woman with a heart of stone.

VIOLA

And I would die a thousand deaths cheerfully, if it made your life easier.

OLIVIA

Where's Cesario going?

VIOLA

Following the one I love more than my eyes or my life. More than I will ever love a wife. That's the truth. The angels in heaven are my witnesses, and can see how pure my love is.

OLIVIA

Ay me, detested! How am I beguiled!

VIOLA

135   Who does beguile you? Who does do you wrong?

OLIVIA

Hast thou forgot thyself? Is it so long?—
Call forth the holy father.

Exit an attendant

ORSINO

(to VIOLA*)*

Come, away!

OLIVIA

Whither, my lord?—Cesario, husband, stay.

ORSINO

Husband?

OLIVIA

Ay, husband. Can he that deny?

ORSINO

140   Her husband, sirrah?

VIOLA

No, my lord, not I.

OLIVIA

Alas, it is the baseness of thy fear
That makes thee strangle thy propriety.
Fear not, Cesario. Take thy fortunes up.
Be that thou know'st thou art, and then thou art
145   As great as that thou fear'st.

Enter PRIEST

O, welcome, father!
Father, I charge thee, by thy reverence,
Here to unfold (though lately we intended
To keep in darkness what occasion now
Reveals before 'tis ripe) what thou dost know
150   Hath newly passed between this youth and me.

OLIVIA

Ah, how awful, I feel so used! I've been tricked!

VIOLA

Who tricked you? Who treated you badly?

OLIVIA

Have you completely forgotten? Has it been so long? Call the priest.

An attendant exits.

ORSINO

(to VIOLA*)* Come on, let's go!

OLIVIA

Go where, my lord?—Cesario, my husband, stay here.

ORSINO

Husband?

OLIVIA

Yes, husband. Can he deny it?

ORSINO

Are you her husband, boy?

VIOLA

No, my lord, not me.

OLIVIA

You're afraid, so you hide your identity. But don't be afraid, Cesario. Accept the good luck that's come your way. Be the person you know you are, and you'll be as powerful as this person you fear.

The PRIEST *enters.*

Oh, hello, father! Father, could I please ask you to tell these people what happened between me and this young man? (I know we wanted to hide it, but now the situation demands that we reveal everything.)

PRIEST
> A contract of eternal bond of love,
> Confirmed by mutual joinder of your hands,
> Attested by the holy close of lips,
> Strengthened by interchangement of your rings,
155 > And all the ceremony of this compact
> Sealed in my function, by my testimony,
> Since when, my watch hath told me, toward my grave
> I have traveled but two hours.

ORSINO
> O thou dissembling cub! What wilt thou be
160 > When time hath sowed a grizzle on thy case?
> Or will not else thy craft so quickly grow
> That thine own trip shall be thine overthrow?
> Farewell, and take her; but direct thy feet
> Where thou and I henceforth may never meet.

VIOLA
165 > My lord, I do protest—

OLIVIA
> O, do not swear!
> Hold little faith, though thou hast too much fear.

Enter SIR ANDREW

SIR ANDREW
> For the love of God, a surgeon! Send one presently to Sir
> Toby.

OLIVIA
> What's the matter?

SIR ANDREW
170 > He has broke my head across and has given Sir Toby a
> bloody coxcomb too. For the love of God, your help! I had
> rather than forty pound I were at home.

OLIVIA
> Who has done this, Sir Andrew?

PRIEST

They were joined in an eternal bond of love and matrimony, and it was confirmed by a holy kiss and an exchange of rings. I witnessed it all as priest. It took place just two hours ago.

ORSINO

(to VIOLA) Oh, you little liar! How much worse will you be when you're older? Maybe you'll get so good at deceit that your tricks will destroy you. Goodbye, and take her. Just never set foot in any place where you and I might happen to meet.

VIOLA

My lord, I swear to you—

OLIVIA

Oh, don't swear! Keep a little bit of honesty, even if you're afraid.

SIR ANDREW *enters.*

SIR ANDREW

For the love of God, call a doctor! Sir Toby needs help right away.

OLIVIA

What's the matter?

SIR ANDREW

He cut my head and gave Sir Toby a bloody head, too. For the love of God, help us! I'd give forty pounds to be safe at home right now.

OLIVIA

Who did this, Sir Andrew?

SIR ANDREW

175   The Count's gentleman, one Cesario. We took him for a
coward, but he's the very devil incardinate.

ORSINO

My gentleman, Cesario?

SIR ANDREW

'Od's lifelings, here he is!—You broke my head for nothing,
and that that I did, I was set on to do 't by Sir Toby.

VIOLA

Why do you speak to me? I never hurt you.
180   You drew your sword upon me without cause,
But I bespoke you fair and hurt you not.

SIR ANDREW

If a bloody coxcomb be a hurt, you have hurt me. I think
you set nothing by a bloody coxcomb.

Enter SIR TOBY BELCH *and* FOOL

Here comes Sir Toby halting. You shall hear more. But if he
185   had not been in drink, he would have tickled you othergates
than he did.

ORSINO

How now, gentleman? How is 't with you?

SIR TOBY BELCH

That's all one: has hurt me, and there's the end on 't. *(to*
FOOL*)* Sot, didst see Dick Surgeon, sot?

FOOL

190   Oh, he's drunk, Sir Toby, an hour agone. His eyes were set
at eight i' the morning.

SIR TOBY BELCH

Then he's a rogue, and a passy-measures pavin. I hate a
drunken rogue.

SIR ANDREW

The count's messenger, Cesario. We thought he was a coward, but he fights like a devil.

ORSINO

My Cesario?

SIR ANDREW

Oh, no, there he is! —You cut my head for no reason. Anything I did to you, I did it because Sir Toby made me.

VIOLA

Why are you talking like this? I never hurt you. You waved your sword at me for no reason, but I was nice to you. I didn't hurt you.

SIR ANDREW

If a bloody head counts as a hurt, then you hurt me. Apparently you think there's nothing unusual about a bloody head.

SIR TOBY BELCH *and the* FOOL *enter.*

Here comes Sir Toby, limping. He'll tell you more of the story. If he hadn't been drunk, he would've really roughed you up.

ORSINO

Hello, sir! How are you?

SIR TOBY BELCH

It doesn't matter how I am: he hurt me, and that's that. *(to* FOOL*)* Fool, have you seen Dick the surgeon?

FOOL

Oh, he's drunk, Sir Toby, for a whole hour now. His eyes started glazing over around eight in the morning.

SIR TOBY BELCH

Then he's no good. I hate no-good drunks.

OLIVIA
Away with him! Who hath made this havoc with them?

SIR ANDREW
195   I'll help you, Sir Toby, because we'll be dressed together.

SIR TOBY BELCH
Will you help?—An ass-head, and a coxcomb, and a knave, a thin-faced knave, a gull!

OLIVIA
Get him to bed, and let his hurt be looked to.

Exeunt FOOL, FABIAN, SIR TOBY BELCH, *and* SIR ANDREW
Enter SEBASTIAN

SEBASTIAN
I am sorry, madam, I have hurt your kinsman,
200   But, had it been the brother of my blood,
I must have done no less with wit and safety.
You throw a strange regard upon me, and by that
I do perceive it hath offended you.
Pardon me, sweet one, even for the vows
205   We made each other but so late ago.

ORSINO
One face, one voice, one habit, and two persons!
A natural perspective, that is and is not!

SEBASTIAN
Antonio, O my dear Antonio!
How have the hours racked and tortured me
210   Since I have lost thee!

ANTONIO
Sebastian are you?

SEBASTIAN
Fear'st thou that, Antonio?

OLIVIA

Take him away! Who did this to him?

SIR ANDREW

I'll help you, Sir Toby. They'll treat our wounds together.

SIR TOBY BELCH

Will you help me?—What an ass and a fool, a gullible no-good idiot!

OLIVIA

Get him to bed and make sure his wounds are treated.

The FOOL, FABIAN, SIR TOBY BELCH,
and SIR ANDREW *exit.*
SEBASTIAN *enters.*

SEBASTIAN

I'm sorry, madam. I wounded your relative. But I would've been forced to do the same thing to my brother, since my safety was at stake. You're looking at me strangely, so I guess you're offended. But please forgive me, darling, for the sake of the vows we made to each other so recently.

ORSINO

One face, one voice, one way of dressing, but two people! It's like an optical illusion. It is and isn't the same person!

SEBASTIAN

Antonio, oh my dear Antonio! I've been so tortured since I lost track of you!

ANTONIO

Are you Sebastian?

SEBASTIAN

Do you have any doubts, Antonio?

ANTONIO
How have you made division of yourself?
An apple, cleft in two, is not more twin
215   Than these two creatures. Which is Sebastian?

OLIVIA
Most wonderful!

SEBASTIAN
(looking at VIOLA*)* Do I stand there? I never had a brother;
Nor can there be that deity in my nature,
Of here and everywhere. I had a sister,
220   Whom the blind waves and surges have devoured.
Of charity, what kin are you to me?
What countryman? What name? What parentage?

VIOLA
Of Messaline. Sebastian was my father;
Such a Sebastian was my brother too,
225   So went he suited to his watery tomb.
If spirits can assume both form and suit
You come to fright us.

SEBASTIAN
                              A spirit I am indeed,
But am in that dimension grossly clad
Which from the womb I did participate.
230   Were you a woman, as the rest goes even,
I should my tears let fall upon your cheek
And say "Thrice-welcome, drownèd Viola!"

VIOLA
My father had a mole upon his brow.

SEBASTIAN
And so had mine.

VIOLA
235   And died that day when Viola from her birth
Had numbered thirteen years.

ANTONIO

How did you divide yourself in two? These two people are as identical as two halves of an apple. Which one is Sebastian?

OLIVIA

How unbelievable!

SEBASTIAN

(*looking at* VIOLA) Is that me standing over there? I never had a brother, and I'm certainly not a god who can be in two places at once. I had a sister who drowned. Please tell me, how am I related to you? Are you from my country? What's your name? Who are your parents?

VIOLA

I'm from Messaline. Sebastian was my father's name, and my brother was named Sebastian too. He was dressed just like you are when he drowned. If ghosts can take on someone's body and clothes, you must be a spirit who's come to frighten us.

SEBASTIAN

I am a spirit, yes, since I have a soul. But my spirit has a body attached to it, one that I've carried since I was in the womb. If you were a woman, I'd hug you now and cry, and say "Welcome back, drowned Viola!"

VIOLA

My father had a mole on his forehead.

SEBASTIAN

Mine did too.

VIOLA

He died on Viola's thirteenth birthday.

SEBASTIAN

Oh, that record is lively in my soul!
He finished indeed his mortal act
That day that made my sister thirteen years.

VIOLA

240 If nothing lets to make us happy both
But this my masculine usurped attire,
Do not embrace me till each circumstance
Of place, time, fortune, do cohere and jump
That I am Viola. Which to confirm,
245 I'll bring you to a captain in this town,
Where lie my maiden weeds, by whose gentle help
I was preserved to serve this noble count.
All the occurrence of my fortune since
Hath been between this lady and this lord.

SEBASTIAN

250 (*to* OLIVIA) So comes it, lady, you have been mistook.
But nature to her bias drew in that.
You would have been contracted to a maid;
Nor are you therein, by my life, deceived.
You are betrothed both to a maid and man.

ORSINO

255 (*to* OLIVIA) Be not amazed. Right noble is his blood.
If this be so, as yet the glass seems true,
I shall have share in this most happy wreck.
(*to* VIOLA) Boy, thou hast said to me a thousand times
Thou never shouldst love woman like to me.

VIOLA

260 And all those sayings will I overswear;
And those swearings keep as true in soul
As doth that orbèd continent the fire
That severs day from night.

ORSINO

Give me thy hand,
And let me see thee in thy woman's weeds.

SEBASTIAN

Oh, I remember that very clearly! It's true, he died on the day my sister turned thirteen.

VIOLA

If the only thing keeping us from rejoicing is the fact that I'm wearing men's clothes, then don't hug me till I can prove beyond the shadow of a doubt that I'm Viola. I'll take you to a sea captain here in town who's got my women's clothing in storage. He saved my life so I could serve this noble count. Everything that's happened to me since then has involved my relationship with this lady and this lord.

SEBASTIAN

(to OLIVIA*)* So you got it wrong, my lady. But nature fixed everything, turning your love for my sister into a love for me. If you hadn't, you would've married a maiden. But that's not completely wrong. I'm still a virgin, so in a sense I'm a maiden too.

ORSINO

(to OLIVIA*)* Don't be shocked. His blood is noble. If this is all as true as it seems to be, then I'm going to have a share in that lucky shipwreck. *(to* VIOLA*)* Boy, you told me a thousand times you'd never love a woman as much as you love me.

VIOLA

Everything I said before I'll say again. I swear I meant every word.

ORSINO

Give me your hand and let me see you dressed in woman's clothing.

VIOLA

265   The captain that did bring me first on shore
         Hath my maid's garments. He, upon some action,
         Is now in durance at Malvolio's suit,
         A gentleman and follower of my lady's.

OLIVIA

         He shall enlarge him.

         Enter FOOL *with a letter, and* FABIAN

270   Fetch Malvolio hither:
         And yet, alas, now I remember me,
         They say, poor gentleman, he's much distract.
         A most extracting frenzy of mine own
         From my remembrance clearly banished his.
275   *(to* FOOL*)* How does he, sirrah?

FOOL

         Truly, madam, he holds Beelzebub at the staves' end as well
         as a man in his case may do. Has here writ a letter to you. I
         should have given 't you today morning, but as a madman's
         epistles are no gospels, so it skills not much when they are
280   delivered.

OLIVIA

         Open 't, and read it.

FOOL

         Look then to be well edified when the fool delivers the
         madman. *(reads)* "By the Lord, madam,"—

OLIVIA

         How now? Art thou mad?

FOOL

285   No, madam, I do but read madness. An your ladyship will
         have it as it ought to be, you must allow *vox.*

OLIVIA

         Prithee, read i' thy right wits.

VIOLA

The captain who brought me to shore has my women's clothes. For some reason he's in prison now on some legal technicality, on Malvolio's orders. Malvolio is a gentleman in my lady's entourage.

OLIVIA

He'll release him.

FABIAN *and the* FOOL *with a letter enter.*

Go and get Malvolio—But, oh no! Now I remember, they say the poor man is mentally ill. I was so crazy myself that I forgot all about him. *(to the* FOOL*)* How is Malvolio doing, do you know?

FOOL

Well, he keeps the devil away as well as a man can in his situation. He's written you a letter. I would've given it to you this morning, but a madman's letters aren't Gospel, so it doesn't matter much if I'm a bit late.

OLIVIA

Open it and read it.

FOOL

There's a lot to learn when a fool recites the words of a madman. *(he reads)* "I swear to God, madam,"—

OLIVIA

Why are you talking like that? Are you insane?

FOOL

No, madam, I'm just reading an insane letter. If you want things done in the right way, you'll have to let me read a crazy letter in a crazy voice.

OLIVIA

No, please, read it like a sane person.

FOOL

So I do, madonna. But to read his right wits is to read thus.
Therefore perpend, my princess, and give ear.

OLIVIA

290   (*giving the letter to* FABIAN) Read it you, sirrah.

FABIAN

(*reads*)

"By the Lord, madam, you wrong me, and the world
shall know it. Though you have put me into darkness and
given your drunken cousin rule over me, yet have I the
benefit of my senses as well as your Ladyship. I have your
295   own letter that induced me to the semblance I put on,
with the which I doubt not but to do myself much right
or you much shame. Think of me as you please. I leave
my duty a little unthought of and speak out of my injury.
The madly used Malvolio."

OLIVIA

300   Did he write this?

FOOL

Ay, madam.

ORSINO

This savors not much of distraction.

OLIVIA

See him delivered, Fabian; bring him hither.

Exit FABIAN

My lord so please you, these things further thought on,
305   To think me as well a sister as a wife,
One day shall crown the alliance on 't, so please you,
Here at my house and at my proper cost.

FOOL

I will, my lady, but a sane person reading this would make it sound crazy. So listen up, princess.

OLIVIA

(giving the letter to FABIAN*)* Oh, you read it, sir.

FABIAN

(he reads)
"I swear to God, madam, you've wronged me, and I'll tell the whole world. You've shut me up in a dark room and given your drunken cousin authority over me, but I'm as sane as you are. I've got a letter from you encouraging me to act the way I did. If I didn't have it, I couldn't prove that I'm right and you're wrong. I don't care what you think of me. I'm going to forget my duties to you a little bit and complain about the injuries you've caused me. Signed,
The poorly treated Malvolio."

OLIVIA

Did he write this?

FOOL

Yes, madam.

ORSINO

It doesn't sound like an insane person's letter.

OLIVIA

Set him free. Fabian, bring him here.

FABIAN *exits.*

My lord, I hope that after you think things over a bit you'll come to like the idea of having me as a sister-in-law instead of a wife. We can have the weddings tomorrow if you want, here at my own house. I'll pay for everything.

ORSINO
> Madam, I am most apt to embrace your offer.
> *(to* VIOLA*)*
> Your master quits you, and for your service done him,
310   So much against the mettle of your sex,
> So far beneath your soft and tender breeding,
> And since you called me "master" for so long,
> Here is my hand. You shall from this time be
> Your master's mistress.

OLIVIA
> *(to* VIOLA*)*   A sister! You are she.

Enter FABIAN, *with* MALVOLIO

ORSINO
315   Is this the madman?

OLIVIA
>   Ay, my lord, this same.
> How now, Malvolio!

MALVOLIO
>   Madam, you have done me wrong,
> Notorious wrong.

OLIVIA
> Have I, Malvolio? No.

MALVOLIO
> *(handing a paper)*
>   Lady, you have. Pray you, peruse that letter.
> You must not now deny it is your hand.
320   Write from it if you can, in hand or phrase;
> Or say 'tis not your seal, not your invention:
> You can say none of this. Well, grant it then
> And tell me, in the modesty of honor,
> Why you have given me such clear lights of favor,
325   Bade me come smiling and cross-gartered to you,
> To put on yellow stockings, and to frown
> Upon Sir Toby and the lighter people?

ORSINO

I accept that offer happily, madam. *(to* VIOLA*)* So you're free now. I'm offering you my hand in marriage because of your loyal service to me, which was far from what any woman should be expected to do, especially a noble woman. You've called me "master" for so long. And now you'll be your master's mistress.

OLIVIA

(to VIOLA*)* You'll be my sister-in-law!

FABIAN *enters with* MALVOLIO.

ORSINO

Is this the madman?

OLIVIA

Yes, my lord. How are you, Malvolio?

MALVOLIO

Madam, you've treated me badly, very badly.

OLIVIA

I did, Malvolio? No.

MALVOLIO

(he hands OLIVIA *a paper)* You did. Please have a look at this letter. You can't deny that it's your handwriting. Go ahead and try to write differently, and try to pretend that's not your seal with your design on it. You can't. So just admit it. And tell me honestly, why did you show me such fondness and asked me to smile at you, wear yellow stockings and crisscrossed laces for you, and be rude to Sir Toby and the servants?

And, acting this in an obedient hope,
Why have you suffered me to be imprisoned,
330   Kept in a dark house, visited by the priest,
And made the most notorious geck and gull
That e'er invention played on? Tell me why.

OLIVIA

Alas, Malvolio, this is not my writing,
Though, I confess, much like the character.
335   But out of question, 'tis Maria's hand.
And now I do bethink me, it was she
First told me thou wast mad, then camest in smiling,
And in such forms which here were presupposed
Upon thee in the letter. Prithee, be content.
340   This practice hath most shrewdly passed upon thee;
But when we know the grounds and authors of it,
Thou shalt be both the plaintiff and the judge
Of thine own cause.

FABIAN

                              Good madam, hear me speak,
And let no quarrel nor no brawl to come
345   Taint the condition of this present hour,
Which I have wonder'd at. In hope it shall not,
Most freely I confess, myself and Toby
Set this device against Malvolio here,
Upon some stubborn and uncourteous parts
350   We had conceived against him. Maria writ
The letter at Sir Toby's great importance,
In recompense whereof he hath married her.
How with a sportful malice it was followed,
May rather pluck on laughter than revenge,
355   If that the injuries be justly weighed
That have on both sides passed.

OLIVIA

(to MALVOLIO*)* Alas, poor fool, how have they baffled thee!

And then tell me why you imprisoned me in a dark house after I followed your instructions perfectly. You made me look like the biggest fool that anybody ever tricked. Tell me why you did it.

OLIVIA

I'm sorry, Malvolio, but this isn't my writing, though I admit it looks like mine. It's definitely Maria's hand-writing. Now that I think about it, Maria was the one who first told me you were insane. That's when you came in smiling at me, dressed up like the letter said, and acting just like it told you to act. Someone has played a very mean trick on you, but when we find out who's responsible, you won't just be the victim, but the judge who sentences the culprit. I promise.

FABIAN

Madam, let me say something. Please don't let squabbles ruin this beautiful and miraculous moment. I confess that Toby and I were the ones who tricked Malvolio because we hated his strict and heavy-handed ways. Sir Toby had Maria wrote that letter, and he married her as a reward. We should just laugh about the whole thing rather than get upset about it, especially if we consider that each of the two parties offended the other equally.

OLIVIA

(to MALVOLIO*)* Oh, poor fool, they've really humiliated you!

FOOL

Why, "some are born great, some achieve greatness, and
some have greatness thrown upon them." I was one, sir, in
360   this interlude, one Sir Topas, sir, but that's all one. *(imitates*
MALVOLIO*)* "By the Lord, fool, I am not mad."—But do you
remember? "Madam, why laugh you at such a barren
rascal; an you smile not, he's gagged?" and thus the
whirligig of time brings in his revenges.

MALVOLIO

365   I'll be revenged on the whole pack of you.

Exit

OLIVIA

He hath been most notoriously abused.

ORSINO

Pursue him and entreat him to a peace.

Some exit

He hath not told us of the captain yet.
When that is known and golden time convents,
370   A solemn combination shall be made
Of our dear souls.—Meantime, sweet sister,
We will not part from hence. Cesario, come,
For so you shall be, while you are a man.
But when in other habits you are seen,
375   Orsino's mistress and his fancy's queen.

Exeunt all, except **FOOL**

FOOL

Well, you know, "some are born great, some achieve greatness, and some have greatness thrust upon them." Anyway, I was part of the trick, sir. I pretended to be a priest named Sir Topas. But what does it matter? *(he imitates* MALVOLIO*)* "I swear, fool, I'm not crazy."—But do you remember what he said about me before? "I'm surprised you enjoy the company of this stupid troublemaker—unless he's got somebody laughing at him, he can't think of anything to say." What goes around comes around.

MALVOLIO

I'll get my revenge on every last one of you.

MALVOLIO exits.

OLIVIA

He really was tricked horribly.

ORSINO

Go after him and try to calm him down a little.

Some exit.

He still hasn't told us about the captain. When that's been taken care of and the time is right, we'll all get married. Until then, we'll stay here, my dear sister-in-law. Cesario, come here. I'll keep calling you Cesario while you're still a man, but when we see you in women's clothes you'll be the queen of my dreams, Orsino's true love.

Everyone exits except the FOOL.

FOOL

(sings)

> When that I was and a little tiny boy,
> With hey, ho, the wind and the rain,
> A foolish thing was but a toy,
> For the rain it raineth every day.

380
> But when I came to man's estate,
> With hey, ho, the wind and the rain,
> 'Gainst knaves and thieves men shut their gate,
> For the rain it raineth every day.

> But when I came, alas! to wive,
385
> With hey, ho, the wind and the rain,
> By swaggering could I never thrive,
> For the rain it raineth every day.

> But when I came unto my beds,
> With hey, ho, the wind and the rain,
390
> With toss-pots still had drunken heads,
> For the rain it raineth every day.

> A great while ago the world begun,
> With hey, ho, the wind and the rain,
> But that's all one, our play is done,
395
> And we'll strive to please you every day.

Exit

FOOL

(he sings)

> When I was a tiny little boy,
> With, hey, ho, the wind and the rain,
> A foolish thing didn't matter much,
> Because the rain it rains every day.
>
> But when I became a man,
> With, hey, ho, the wind and the rain,
> People stopped talking to bad guys and thieves.
> Because the rain it rains every day.
>
> But when I got married, ah, too bad!
> With, hey, ho, the wind and the rain,
> It did me no good to boast and show off,
> Because the rain, it rains every day.
>
> But when I had to go to bed
> With, hey, ho, the wind and the rain,
> With idiots drunk out of their minds,
> Because the rain it rains every day.
>
> The world began a long time ago,
> With, hey, ho, the wind and the rain,
> But that doesn't matter, our play is done,
> And we'll try to please you every day.

*The **FOOL** exits.*

SPARKNOTES LITERATURE GUIDES

1984
The Adventures of
  Huckleberry Finn
The Adventures of Tom
  Sawyer
The Aeneid
All Quiet on the Western
  Front
And Then There Were
  None
Angela's Ashes
Animal Farm
Anna Karenina
Anne of Green Gables
Anthem
Antony and Cleopatra
Aristotle's Ethics
As I Lay Dying
As You Like It
Atlas Shrugged
The Autobiography of
  Malcolm X
The Awakening
The Bean Trees
The Bell Jar
Beloved
Beowulf
Billy Budd
Black Boy
Bless Me, Ultima
The Bluest Eye
Brave New World
The Brothers Karamazov
The Call of the Wild
Candide
The Canterbury Tales
Catch-22
The Catcher in the Rye
The Chocolate War
The Chosen
Cold Mountain
Cold Sassy Tree
The Color Purple
The Count of Monte
  Cristo
Crime and Punishment
The Crucible
Cry, the Beloved Country
Cyrano de Bergerac

David Copperfield
Death of a Salesman
The Death of Socrates
The Diary of a Young Girl
A Doll's House
Don Quixote
Dr. Faustus
Dr. Jekyll and Mr. Hyde
Dracula
Dune
Edith Hamilton's
  Mythology
Emma
Ethan Frome
Fahrenheit 451
Fallen Angels
A Farewell to Arms
Farewell to Manzanar
Flowers for Algernon
For Whom the Bell Tolls
The Fountainhead
Frankenstein
The Giver
The Glass Menagerie
Gone With the Wind
The Good Earth
The Grapes of Wrath
Great Expectations
The Great Gatsby
Grendel
Gulliver's Travels
Hamlet
The Handmaid's Tale
Hard Times
Harry Potter and the
  Sorcerer's Stone
Heart of Darkness
Henry IV, Part I
Henry V
Hiroshima
The Hobbit
The House of Seven
  Gables
I Know Why the Caged
  Bird Sings
The Iliad
Inferno
Inherit the Wind
Invisible Man

Jane Eyre
Johnny Tremain
The Joy Luck Club
Julius Caesar
The Jungle
The Killer Angels
King Lear
The Last of the Mohicans
Les Miserables
A Lesson Before Dying
The Little Prince
Little Women
Lord of the Flies
The Lord of the Rings
Macbeth
Madame Bovary
A Man for All Seasons
The Mayor of
  Casterbridge
The Merchant of Venice
A Midsummer Night's
  Dream
Moby Dick
Much Ado About Nothing
My Antonia
Narrative of the Life of
  Frederick Douglass
Native Son
The New Testament
Night
Notes from Underground
The Odyssey
The Oedipus Plays
Of Mice and Men
The Old Man and the Sea
The Old Testament
Oliver Twist
The Once and Future
  King
One Day in the Life of
  Ivan Denisovich
One Flew Over the
  Cuckoo's Nest
One Hundred Years of
  Solitude
Othello
Our Town
The Outsiders
Paradise Lost

A Passage to India
The Pearl
The Picture of Dorian
  Gray
Poe's Short Stories
A Portrait of the Artist as
  a Young Man
Pride and Prejudice
The Prince
A Raisin in the Sun
The Red Badge of
  Courage
The Republic
Richard III
Robinson Crusoe
Romeo and Juliet
The Scarlet Letter
A Separate Peace
Silas Marner
Sir Gawain and the Green
  Knight
Slaughterhouse-Five
Snow Falling on Cedars
Song of Solomon
The Sound and the Fury
Steppenwolf
The Stranger
Streetcar Named Desire
The Sun Also Rises
A Tale of Two Cities
The Taming of the Shrew
The Tempest
Tess of the d'Urbervilles
The Things They Carried
Their Eyes Were
  Watching God
Things Fall Apart
To Kill a Mockingbird
To the Lighthouse
Treasure Island
Twelfth Night
Ulysses
Uncle Tom's Cabin
Walden
War and Peace
Wuthering Heights
A Yellow Raft in Blue
  Water